LOW-PROT

A wide range of recipes and soun
a low-protein diet can be d

In the same series

GLUTEN-FREE COOKING
HIGH-FIBRE COOKING
LOW-FAT AND NO-FAT COOKING
SALT-FREE COOKING
WHEAT-FREE, MILK-FREE, EGG-FREE COOKING

LOW-PROTEIN COOKING

by

SARAH BOUNDS

Illustrated by Ian Jones

THORSONS PUBLISHERS LIMITED
Wellingborough, Northamptonshire

First published 1983

British Library Cataloguing in Publication Data

Bounds, Sarah
Low-protein cooking.
1. Low-protein diet — Recipes
I. Title
641.5'638 RM237.9

ISBN 0-7225-0828-X

Printed in Great Britain by
Richard Clay (The Chaucer Press) Ltd,
Bungay, Suffolk

CONTENTS

INTRODUCTION

Low-protein cookery need not be dull. By restricting the use of foods rich in protein and by liberally using fresh vegetables, fruits, herbs and spices it is easy to create dishes which are varied and nutritious.

In Britain most of us eat far more protein than we need; we could quite easily cut down on the amount of protein we eat and in doing so would lower the level of fat too. The recipes in this book do just that; they are low in protein and fat, but are high in unrefined carbohydrates and fibre to form the basis of a healthy diet for all.

All the recipes in this book are vegetarian and because cheese and eggs are high in protein, they are restricted; many of the recipes are suitable for vegans too.

1.
ALL ABOUT PROTEIN

Every cell in the body is composed of protein. Proteins give structure to bones, hair, nails and teeth. They are the basis of muscles and internal organs, the heart, kidney and liver. They are the chemistry underlying the hormones, enzymes and blood. Protein is the very essence of life, equally important to plants and animals as to man.

Not surprisingly a substance with such vital importance is itself extremely complex. There are many different types of proteins, each made up of amino acids. There are twenty different amino acids, each with a slightly different composition. All contain nitrogen, oxygen, hydrogen and carbon and some also contain sulphur. These basic elements joined together in different sequences make up individual amino acids. And these amino acids in turn link to form long chains — proteins. Each protein is like a word, but so complicated is its spelling, it could have several thousand letters.

The proteins in the body are constantly in use; they are subjected to continual wear and tear and they need replacing when worn out. In growing children tissues are constantly being formed and proteins laid down as the body grows and develops.

The body is able to build its own proteins as required. But to do so it needs a constant supply of amino acids. So we need to obtain amino acids from the food we eat to give the body basic building blocks for protein synthesis. Amino acids in the diet are supplied by protein in the food we eat. The body digests the protein from food and splits each protein into amino acids. The cells of the body then select the amino acids required to build new proteins.

The process of replenishment or repairing worn out body proteins and laying down new proteins is constant. Every moment of the day more proteins are being worn out and need replacing — so we must ensure that the body has sufficient amino acids to synthesize new proteins.

How much do we need?

We need sufficient protein in the diet to cover the losses of protein from the body. Every ten days half the heart, liver and kidney have been replaced. Every five to six months half the muscle, skin and bones have been replaced. Adults need enough protein from their diet to cover these protein losses, supplying adequate amino acids for the synthesis of new body proteins.

Babies, children and pregnant women all need more than this basic 'replenishment' protein. Extra protein is required for the laying down of new proteins in the developing foetus and child.

The body must be in a state of nitrogen balance. The nitrogen lost in the protein broken down and removed from the body through the skin, urine and faeces should equal what is being taken in in food.

Despite the fact that the need for protein is well understood there are conflicting opinions as to just what that means in grams of protein needed in the diet each day.

On the one hand there are those who say that only 0.5g protein per kg body weight is required each day by an adult — on the other hand there are those who recommend amounts far above this level.

On this basis an average man weighing 70kg, would need 35g protein a day. Experiments have shown that men can live perfectly healthily on an intake of no more than 40g protein a day. Many societies survive on such low intakes. Despite this evidence, for many years the figure used in assessing the adequacy of diets was one gram of protein per kg body weight per day, suggesting that the average 70kg man would need 70g protein each day. Today guidelines from the Food and Agriculture Organization (FAO) and World Health Organization (WHO) recommend a minimum level which works out at around 40g a day for the average male and 56g a day as a safe level.

In practice, ten per cent of the total energy value of the diet is often used to set the recommended level of protein (DHSS). This is an important aspect of assessing the adequacy of diets. Experience in the underdeveloped Third World nations has shown that in many cases it is more important to supply an adequate amount of food to meet energy needs, rather than giving protein rich supplements. If there is sufficient fat and carbohydrate to fuel the body's energy needs, then protein will be used for energy and not for vital repair and growth processes.

Children need proportionately more protein than adults because of the need for extra protein in the growing body. Around 20g a day is needed for the first three months of life. An extra ten per cent of an adult's requirement is added to the needs of pregnant women.

In 1980 the average British diet supplied 72.7g protein per person per day (National Food Survey) — well over the advisory limits. It is normal for the diets of wealthy nations such as ours to supply more protein (and of course more food generally) than we need. Obesity is said to be one of our major health problems, with around forty per cent of the population overweight. Eating more protein than we need does not have any advantages. Slimming diets where a high protein intake is recommended work only in the short term because they dispel a little water from the body which leads to a loss of a few pounds. If the body does take in more protein than it needs to meet repair and growth processes, the protein is used to supply energy. And if energy needs have also already been met then the amino acids, surplus to requirements, will be stored for later use for energy along with surplus fat and carbohydrate. In time, stores build up and the person gains weight — obesity results.

Because it is normal for the British diet to supply more protein than required, the term low-protein can be misleading. When a doctor or specialist recommends a low-protein diet often it is simply a question of reducing the protein level to the minimum requirement, around 40g a day. Rarely is a figure below this advised except to patients severely ill in hospital where they can be supervised. So if you've been advised to follow a low-protein diet, there is no need to panic! By careful choice of foods it is easy to keep protein intake within certain limits, and easy to eat well too.

Who needs a low-protein diet?

There are several specific illnesses or health problems where a low-protein diet may be recommended. There is also good evidence that we could all benefit by switching our diet from one that in Britain is likely to be high in fat, protein and refined carbohydrates to one that is ostensibly lower in fat and higher in unrefined carbohydrates and which will contain a lower but perfectly adequate intake of protein.

Kidney disease is perhaps the most common complaint where a restriction of protein intake can prove beneficial. When protein is broken down during digestion the waste products are removed from the body via the kidneys. So when the kidney is damaged or functioning below par, then it is quite logical to reduce its workload.

Kidney problems where protein may be restricted are:

1. Acute nephritic syndrome. This often occurs after an infection like scarlet fever or tonsillitis caused by streptococcal bacteria.
2. Acute renal failure
3. Chronic renal failure
4. Haemodialysis

In contrast to these kidney problems where limiting the protein intake can be beneficial, is the nephritic syndrome where dietary protein is increased to correct the large loss of protein that occurs with the condition.

A large amount of protein in the diet, particularly from foods high in purines like sea food, liver and kidneys, can aggravate gout. As the purines are broken down the levels of uric acid are increased; it is uric acid that can bring on an attack in gouty people.

Low-protein diets are often vital to infants born with faulty metabolism. There are more than fifty conditions where there is a defect in the body's enzyme system responsible for metabolizing amino acids. A shortage or total absence of an enzyme needed to metabolize an individual amino acid means that it cannot be properly used in the body. Many of these inborn errors in metabolism of amino acids are extremely rare; phenylketonuria (PKU) is one more common than most. It is due to a genetic deficiency of phenylalanine hydroxylase, the enzyme essential for converting phenylalanine to tyrosine. There is a build up of the amino acid and substances related to it which can affect the brain, causing severe and possibly irreversible damage. Treatment of these conditions is based on a diet that is usually low in protein, with a restriction of the amino acid affected in each case.

What happens if we don't get enough?

Cutting down the protein level of the diet might run the risk of a shortage. If the body uses more protein than is being replaced in the diet then an imbalance occurs. The cells of the body lack the amino acids required for the synthesis of new proteins.

In a young child there is quite simply a failure to grow. Growth and development are slowed down by the shortage of the vital amino acids needed for new tissue formation.

In adults and children alike the first areas of the body to suffer are those where the protein is quickly turned over. This is fastest in the lining of the intestine and in the glands which secrete digestive enzymes. So the first sign of a deficiency of protein is a failure to digest and absorb food, leading to diarrhoea. Gradually the liver fails to work normally, fat starts to build up in the liver cells. Muscles begin to be destroyed as the body withdraws the protein.

In underdeveloped nations shortages of protein in the diet are often closely linked to a general shortage of food, limiting the energy intake. Whenever there is insufficient fat and carbohydrate (the two main energy sources), protein goes to produce energy at the expense of the synthesis of proteins for growth and repair.

Two conditions could result — *marasmus*, where there is a shortage of both protein and energy, and *kwashiorkor*, where there is simply a protein shortage. Both are common in poor underdeveloped nations.

It's not just the quantity . . .

While the amount of protein supplied in the diet is important there is another vital factor to consider; the question of quality. Protein quality determines how useful the protein is to the body and is expressed in terms of the amino acids found in food.

Eight of the twenty amino acids are said to be essential. The body is able to make the other twelve from these basic eight essential amino acids. Complex processes of conversion enable these basic eight to be subsequently used to produce other amino acids as required by the body.

The protein quality of a food indicates the presence or absence of these essential amino acids and also considers the amount of each present. The body has varying needs for each; ideally protein should supply all the essential amino acids in the quantities needed by the body.

The eight essential amino acids are:

valine
leucine
isoleucine
threonine
lysine
phenylalanine
methionine
tryptophan

Histidine is essential for children.

The biological value of the food expresses its amino acid profile in terms of its usefulness to the body. It is calculated by considering the amount of nitrogen retained by the body and the amount absorbed. This indicates how much is used and so indicates how close it comes to supplying the eight essential amino acids in the correct proportions.

The food that comes closest to the ideal protein is the egg. With a biological value of 97 it is above other animal and plant foods. The lower the biological value the greater the gap there is between what the body needs and what the protein in that food supplies. Ideally every meal should provide a perfect balance of amino acids, and fortunately nature helps us out! The proteins in different types of food vary; where one food might be low in one particular amino acid, another will supply this in adequate amounts. *Combining different foods together complements the protein quality of each, giving an all round balanced protein intake.*

Mixing different ingredients together is second nature, to eat just one food would be extremely boring and not good for the body either. We mix different foods together to give interesting meals and a varied diet, and often unconsciously to meet the body's nutritive needs. So when we grab a quick cheese sandwich for lunch we are balancing the amino acids in the cheese with those in the bread and are giving the body a perfect balance of amino acids to build new proteins.

Protein quality becomes even more important on a low-protein diet. Careful planning and consideration of the foods chosen is needed to ensure that foods are being combined to make the most efficient use of the protein in the diet. It is important that all the essential amino acids be present at each meal to ensure that the best use is made of them.

If the body does not receive all the eight essential amino acids it needs at one meal then there is the danger that some will be wasted. Rather like an impatient child who can't find a missing piece of jigsaw, he breaks up the puzzle and throws the pieces aside in disgust. The body, short of an essential amino acid, is unable to synthesize new proteins and those amino acids present will be wasted.

2.

PLANNING A LOW-PROTEIN DIET

The aim of a low-protein diet is to supply the body with just enough protein to meet the body's needs and with the right balance of amino acids. But protein must never be considered in isolation. Because you are told to cut down on protein it doesn't mean ignore the rest of your diet. It is always important to look at your diet as a whole, to ensure that all the nutrients needed for health to be maintained are present — and present in the correct amounts.

With the exception of white sugar, which is purely carbohydrate, foods do not contain just one nutrient alone; they contain a mixture of various substances. Watching what you eat, from a protein point of view, affects your intake of other nutrients and vice versa. The relative contribution played by the three energy-producing nutrients (fats, carbohydrates and proteins) can have serious implications for health.

A low-protein diet should supply the body with just enough protein to meet the body's needs. The eight essential amino acids and the other nutrients required by the body should be present in adequate quantities. The other nutrients needed by the body are:

Fat — some fat must be present in the diet to supply essential fatty acids which are needed for many basic body functions. The essential fatty acids (linolenic acid and linoleic acid) are both found in vegetable oils, and are polyunsaturated fatty acids (PUFA). PUFA are also said to be important in protecting against heart disease. Whereas vegetable oils and fats tend to be either PUFA or monounsaturated fatty acids, animal fats tend to be saturated. There is evidence (still hotly contested by some) that PUFA can help to prevent the silting up of the arteries (arteriosclerosis) that leads to heart disease. PUFA can lower the amount of fat circulating in the blood and so lower the risk that some of this blood fat might be deposited on the artery walls. Saturated fatty acids do not exert this protective influence. It seems logical therefore to try to cut down on the amount of saturated fat and switch instead to PUFA. Because fat is a highly concentrated form of energy, it is generally desirable to cut the total level of fat in the diet — relying more heavily on unrefined carbohydrates.

Carbohydrates — a whole family of substances ranging from the simplest sugars like glucose to the more complex starch. Also included under the general term carbohydrates is dietary fibre, because it is made up of very complicated carbohydrates, so complex that the human body cannot break them down. Fibre therefore passes through the body undigested, and that is the key to its function in the body. While the other carbohydrates are broken down to supply energy for the body's physical activities and metabolism, dietary fibre passes through the system adding bulk to the diet. It helps promote a healthy digestion by making the contents of the intestines flow more smoothly and be eliminated more quickly. Constipation is averted and a whole host of other diseases are now thought to be prevented, at least in part, by the presence of fibre in the diet.

A look at underdeveloped nations revealed that their diets were higher in fibre than those of wealthy developed countries like Britain. Researchers found the pattern of disease typical in each was different too. The diseases which are common in our country are rare in underdeveloped nations. Now evidence is growing that an adequate intake of fibre in the diet can help to prevent more than just constipation, but diseases as diverse as diabetes, colonic cancer, appendicitis, and hiatus hernia.

The process of refining carbohydrates removes much of the fibre from food (as well as vital vitamins and minerals). So swap white bread for wholemeal, white pasta for the tastier wholemeal varieties and white rice for brown. Eliminating highly refined carbohydrates is a vital step to take towards health.

Vitamins — are substances needed to carry out vital body processes. They are required in quite small amounts, but can easily be lost by processing techniques as well as careless cooking. Here is a brief summary of the actions of each in the body:

Vitamin A — healthy eyesight and protection against infection.
Vitamin B group — for the release of energy from food and for a healthy nervous system.
Vitamin C — to fight infection and for the smooth running of many vital body processes.
Vitamin D — for healthy bones and teeth.
Vitamin E — to exert a protective effect within the body.

Minerals — at least sixteen mineral elements are needed by the body. Some, like calcium and potassium, are needed in relatively large amounts, others, like iron and selenium, are required in tiny concentrations, but can be just as difficult, if not more so, to secure in adequate amounts.

The typical British diet relies heavily on fat and refined carbohydrates plus protein to supply energy. If your diet fits that picture then cut down on the amount of fat, switch from animal fats to vegetable fats and replace refined carbohydrates with unrefined. The first step towards achieving this, and of course a lower protein content, is to cut out or cut down dramatically on the amount of meat you eat.

We assume that meat is the perfect protein food. But in meat the protein comes hand in hand with saturated fats and there is no fibre. Modern methods of farming rely heavily on hormones and antibiotics to rear animals for slaughter. The feed used by farmers is more than likely to contain insecticides and pesticides as well as traces of chemical fertilizer. All these chemicals build up within the flesh of the animal and are passed on to our bodies as the meat is digested. What began as traces of chemicals, can over a long period build up in our tissues into more significant amounts with inherent dangers. In addition there are many who object to meat eating on ethical grounds, questioning the right of man to kill for his stomach in a society where there are plenty of plant alternatives. There is also the ecological question, the fairness of an agricultural system that feeds crops, which could often be eaten direct by man, to livestock for subsequent food for us. It is a wasteful, extravagant system, all the more so in the context of the continuing food problems facing Third World nations battling against starvation. An acre of land planted with cereal crops could produce five times as much protein as one devoted to livestock and one planted with legumes (beans, peas and lentils) ten times as much.

Like meat, fish contains around twenty per cent protein and as such is difficult to justify in a low-protein diet. It is hard to limit portion size to keep down the protein level per serving. Many also reject fish on humane grounds, and again there is the threat of chemical contamination of the flesh from pollutants — mercury being a prime example. Cheese also has a high protein level but can be used sparingly to contribute both flavour and colour to a dish. Two ounces of cheese in a dish for four people goes a long way — the same amount of fish would be lost and would probably pass unnoticed! One disadvantage of cheese however, like all dairy produce, is its high level of saturated fat. Skimmed milk and cheeses are a sensible alternative and are becoming more widely available. Yogurt is another useful ingredient; made from skimmed milk it has a tanginess which can contribute much to the flavour of a dish. Yogurt also contains certain bacteria which help digestion.

The recipes you will find in this book blend dairy produce with plant proteins, vegetables and fruits. The emphasis is firmly on plant sources of protein to supply the essential amino acids, with smaller amounts of dairy produce to help complement the plant proteins.

Complementary Proteins

Plant proteins have a lower biological value than animal proteins but are lower in fat (with the exception of nuts), they tend to contain PUFA rather than saturated fatty acids, supply dietary fibre and also contain vitamins and minerals. Deficiencies of amino acids in one plant food can be made good by mixing with another. Conveniently, plants which are valuable sources of protein fall into three distinct groups:

cereal grains, including rice, wheat, rye, millet and barley;

pulses including beans, peas and lentils;
nuts and seeds including sunflower and sesame seeds as well as the numerous nut varieties.

Each group has a characteristic make-up of amino acids and tends to be short of a particular amino acid. By mixing two of the three groups of plant foods together at one meal you obtain a balanced intake.

The mixing is often already carried out for us in recipes — instinct tells us to blend different ingredients together to make meals more appetizing — and for once our instincts are right! Traditional dishes carry out protein combining perfectly. In India for example, lentils or split peas are curried and served with rice or a bread made from wheat flour.

From a culinary and nutritional point of view the best vegetarian dishes are those that combine different plant protein foods with vegetables and with each other, or alternatively with dairy products to supply the body not only with a balanced protein intake but also with a relatively low level of fat, fibre, energy-producing carbohydrates and with vitamins and minerals. This is the basis of my book. By carefully limiting the use of protein rich ingredients, but combining together different protein foods with ample vegetables which are lower in protein, the protein in each and every dish is carefully regulated to form part of an appealing and appetizing low-protein diet.

A TYPICAL DAY'S EATING

A low-protein diet needn't be boring — follow the recipes in this book and you can feed all the family. Simply add a little of the higher protein foods for children, adolescents and pregnant and lactating mothers, all of whom need more protein than most. If you have been put on a low-protein diet by your doctor, ask him how much protein in grams to eat each day. For convenience, each recipe has an approximate protein content and calorie value per serving. Remember to use different ingredients to make meals interesting and remember to follow the simple protein combining rules. A typical day's menu should follow this simple regime:

Breakfast

Choose a protein balanced combination with enough calories to keep your blood sugar level up through the morning for maximum concentration.

Pick from
- — muesli made from cereal flakes, nuts, seeds, dried or fresh fruit;
- — dried fruit compote or fresh fruit with yogurt followed by wholemeal toast;
- — porridge.

Lunch or Light Evening Meal

Choose from
- — soup plus bread roll;
- — salad or mixture of different salads with roll or wholewheat crispbreads;
- — vegetable pastie;
- — a filled baked potato;
- — vegetable pâté e.g., aubergine (eggplant) and chick pea (garbanzo bean) pâté, served with strips of raw vegetables.

Follow with fresh fruit or with yogurt.

Main Meal

Choose a main course taking care not to repeat ingredients used earlier — if leek soup were eaten for lunch, don't then eat leek quiche for supper. Serve, where appropriate, with a side salad or lightly cooked vegetable and follow with a suitable sweet. Balance a heavy main course with a light dessert of fresh fruit or finish a light main course with a richer sweet.

Snacks: try to avoid eating too many in-between nibbles. If you are hungry then choose fresh fruit or raw vegetables to nibble on to keep down your protein intake and calories intake too. Avoid protein-rich nuts and seeds for snacks.

Drinks: avoid drinking too much caffeine loaded tea and coffee. Pick instead decaffeinated coffee and teas with less caffeine (and tannin).

Watch how much milk you add — try drinking it black. Mineral waters are a suitable substitute. Fruit juices supply protein so don't be too generous with juice. Remember that orange and pineapple both supply 0.4g per 100ml, grapefruit 0.3g and tomato juice 0.7g per 100ml. Alcoholic drinks also supply protein — beer contains 0.3g protein per 100ml, so a pint supplies 1.8g. Wine supplies 0.1-0.2g per 100ml. Spirits and cider contain only a trace.

3.
THE PROTEIN CONTENT OF FOODS

To help you learn the protein values of different foods, here is a list of foods with the percentage of protein each contains. (Figures taken from McCance and Widdowson's *The Composition of Foods* and the US Department of Agriculture Handbook of the Nutritional Contents of Foods.)

Vegetables
(*Figures for raw produce unless otherwise stated.*)

artichokes (Jerusalem)	1.6	cauliflower	1.9
asparagus	1.7	celery	0.9
aubergine (eggplant)	0.7	cucumber	1.9
french (snap) beans		leeks	1.8
(boiled)	0.8	lettuce	1.0
runner (green) beans		marrow (squash)	0.4
(boiled)	1.9	mushrooms	1.8
broad (Windsor) beans		onions	0.9
(boiled)	4.1	parsnips	1.7
haricot (navy) beans	21.4	peas	5.8
beansprouts	1.6	green peppers	0.9
broccoli	3.1	potatoes	2.1
brussels sprouts (boiled)	2.8	spinach, boiled	5.1
red cabbage	1.7	swede (rutabaga)	1.1
savoy	3.3	sweetcorn kernels	4.1
spring cabbage (boiled)	1.1	tomatoes	0.9
white cabbage	1.9	turnips	0.8
carrots	0.6-0.9	watercress	2.9

Cereals

oatmeal	12.4	wheatgerm	26.5
rice	6.5	wholemeal flour	13.2
rye flour	8.2	wholemeal pasta (from Record Foods)	13.9
wheat bran	14.1		

Nuts and Seeds

almonds	16.9	peanuts	24.3
brazils	12.0	sesame seeds	18.6
cashews	17.2	sunflower seeds	24.0
chestnuts	2.0	walnuts	10.6
hazelnuts	7.6		

Dried Pulses

chick peas	20.2	lentils	23.8
haricot beans	21.4	split dried peas	22.1
red kidney	22.1		

Dairy Foods

cottage cheese	13.6	egg yolk	16.1
Cheddar	26.0	skim milk	3.4
Edam	24.0	whole milk	3.3
whole egg	12.3	yogurt	5.0
egg white	9.0		

Meat, Fish and Poultry

(*Figures for lean meat.*)

bacon	20.2	mackerel	19.0
beef	20.3	ox liver	21.1
chicken	20.5	pork	20.7
cod	17.4	prawns	22.6
lamb	20.8	trout	23.5
lamb's kidney	16.5	tuna	22.8
lamb's liver	20.1	turkey	21.9

Fruit

apples	0.3	oranges	0.8
apricots (fresh)	0.6	peaches	0.6
apricots (dried)	4.8	pears	0.2
blackberries	1.3	plums	0.6
blackcurrants	0.8	prunes	2.4
dried currants	1.7	raisins	1.1
dried dates	2.0	raspberries	0.9
gooseberries	1.1	rhubarb	0.6
grapes, black	0.6	sultanas	1.8
grapefruit	0.6	water melon	0.4
honeydew melon	0.6		

4.
BASICS

WHOLEMEAL BREAD

Makes 2 small loaves or 20 rolls. Supplies around 3g protein/85 calories per thick slice or roll.

Bread doesn't need to be left out of a low-protein diet — the fibre contained in wholemeal bread helps to fill you up, so you eat less. It also supplies essential vitamins and minerals missing from refined flours. Adding vitamin C to the basic breadmaking recipe cuts down on the lengthy proving process.

Imperial (Metric)
1 oz (25g) soft vegetable margarine
1½ lb (⅔ kilo) wholemeal flour
1 teaspoonful sea salt
1 oz (25g) fresh yeast
¾ pint (400ml) tepid water
1 teaspoonful clear honey
25mg vitamin C tablet

American
2½ tablespoonsful soft vegetable margarine
6 cupsful wholewheat flour
1 teaspoonful sea salt
2½ tablespoonsful fresh yeast
2 cupsful tepid water
1 teaspoonful clear honey
25mg vitamin C tablet

1. Rub margarine into flour and salt.
2. Crumble yeast into tepid water, stir in the honey and crush the vitamin C tablet — stir in well and then add to flour mixture.
3. Using your hands mix liquid in thoroughly, drawing in the flour from the sides of the bowl. Knead together and then turn onto a board or table top.

4. Continue to knead for further 10 minutes, adding more flour if necessary. The dough should be soft and smooth, not sticky.

5. Place an upturned bowl on top of dough and leave to rest for 10 minutes.

6. While dough is resting, lightly grease 2 × 1 lb loaf tins or 2 baking sheets.

7. If making loaves divide dough into 2, press out lightly into an oblong, three times as wide as the tin, but the same length. Fold into three and place in tin with seam underneath. Cover and leave in a warm place to double, about 40 minutes. Glaze with milk or beaten egg and bake in a preheated oven 450°F/230°C (Gas Mark 8) for 30 minutes until golden brown. Tip loaf out of tin and, if it sounds hollow when tapped, the loaf is ready.

   If making rolls, divide the dough into 20 equal-sized pieces — shape and place on baking trays. Cover and leave to double in size in a warm place — about 15-20 minutes. Glaze and bake, as above, for 15 minutes until the rolls sound hollow and are golden brown.

MUESLI

Serves 4. Supplies 4.5g protein/200 calories per portion.

A mixture of grains, nuts and dried fruit topped with fresh fruit and moistened with fruit juice makes a simple protein balanced breakfast dish.

Imperial (Metric)	American
4 oz (100g) oat, wheat or rye flakes	2 cupsful of oat, wheat or rye flakes
1 oz (25g) chopped almonds	¼ cupful chopped almonds
2 oz (50g) sultanas	⅓ cupful golden seedless raisins
2 eating apples	2 eating apples
¼ pint (150ml) orange juice	⅔ cupful orange juice

Mix the flakes, nuts and sultanas (golden seedless raisins). Peel, core and finely chop the apples and mix with the other ingredients. Pour over juice and serve.

NATURAL YOGURT

Makes 1 pint of yogurt. Supplies 20.4g protein/198 calories if made from skimmed milk, 19.8g protein/390 calories if made from full fat pasteurized milk.

Making your own yogurt at home is not only cheaper it is also very simple. There is no need to buy an expensive yogurt maker, results are just as good when yogurt is made in a wide necked thermos flask. All you need is a thermometer, to give the right temperature to let the desirable bacteria work and to kill off harmful bacteria.

Use skimmed milk in preference to standard pasteurized or long life milk as the fat has been removed. This gives a lower calorie yogurt.

Use a little yogurt as a starter to supply the necessary bacteria. Once you have made one batch, remember to keep a little to use for the next batch. Start by buying a carton of natural yogurt; make sure that the yogurt is not sterilized, pasteurized or long-life as these processes will have killed the special bacteria needed to produce yogurt. Stir in fresh fruit just before serving — don't store with fresh fruit in the yogurt as the fruit might produce moulds in the mixture and spoil the yogurt.

Imperial (Metric)	American
1 pint (½ litre) skimmed milk	2½ cupsful skimmed milk
1 tablespoonful skimmed milk powder (optional)	1 tablespoonful skimmed milk powder (optional)
1 tablespoonful natural yogurt	1 tablespoonful natural yogurt

1. Place milk in a saucepan and heat gently to 110°F (50°C).
2. While milk is warming, mix yogurt and milk powder (if used) to a smooth paste (the powder gives a slightly thicker yogurt).
3. Pour milk onto the yogurt starter and stir thoroughly. Transfer to a wide-necked vacuum flask and seal.
4. Leave to incubate for 6 to 8 hours then place in fridge to chill before serving.

5.

SOUPS

ARTICHOKE SOUP

Serves 4. Supplies 3g protein/72 calories per portion.

Imperial (Metric)	American
1½ lb (¾ kilo) Jerusalem artichokes	1½ pounds Jerusalem artichokes
1 tablespoonful oil	1 tablespoonful oil
½ lb (¼ kilo) leeks	8 ounces leeks
1½ pints (¾ litre) vegetable stock	3¾ cupsful vegetable stock
Bay leaf	Bay leaf
Sea salt	Sea salt
Freshly ground black pepper	Freshly ground black pepper

1. Place the artichokes in a pan with water. Cook for 15 minutes. Drain and peel.
2. Trim the leeks and slice thinly. Cook in the oil for 2 minutes, then add the artichokes, stock and bay leaf. Bring to the boil, cover and simmer for 35 minutes.
3. Remove bay leaf and liquidize soup. Return to heat, season to taste and serve.

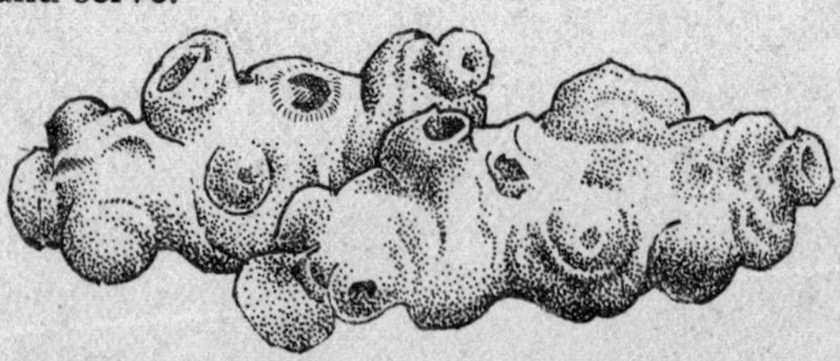

CARROT AND TOMATO SOUP

Serves 4. Supplies 1.8g protein/55 calories per portion.

A hearty, low-protein soup, loaded with vitamin A.

Imperial (Metric)	**American**
1 large onion	1 large onion
2 cloves garlic	2 cloves garlic
3 large carrots, scrubbed and diced	3 large carrots, scrubbed and diced
1 tablespoonful olive oil	1 tablespoonful olive oil
1 lb (½ kilo) fresh tomatoes or 15 oz (425g) tin	1 pound tomatoes or a medium can
½ teaspoonful marjoram	½ teaspoonful marjoram
Bay leaf	Bay leaf
1½ pints (¾ litre) stock	3¾ cupsful stock
Sea salt	Sea salt
Freshly ground black pepper	Freshly ground black pepper
Chopped parsley	Chopped parsley

1. Finely chop the onion and crush the garlic. *Sauté* together with the carrots in the oil for 5 minutes over a low heat.

2. Add the tomatoes (skinned if using fresh), marjoram and bay leaf and the stock. Bring to the boil, then reduce heat to a steady simmer and cook for 30 minutes until the carrots are quite soft.

3. Remove the bay leaf and liquidize the soup. Return to pan and heat through. Season to taste.

CAULIFLOWER SOUP

Serves 4. Supplies 4g protein/100 calories per portion.

A delicate creamy-coloured soup with a beautifully smooth texture.

Imperial (Metric)	American
1 small cauliflower	1 small cauliflower
1 large onion	1 large onion
1 large potato	1 large potato
1 tablespoonful oil	1 tablespoonful oil
1¼ pints (650ml) water	3 cupsful water
2 bay leaves	2 bay leaves
Pinch dried rosemary	Pinch dried rosemary
¼ pint (150ml) milk	⅔ cupful milk
Sea salt	Sea salt
Freshly ground black pepper	Freshly ground black pepper
Chopped chives or parsley to garnish	Chopped chives or parsley to garnish

1. Break cauliflower into florets. Finely chop the onion and peel and dice the potato. Cook all together in the oil for a few minutes.
2. Add water and herbs plus milk. Bring to the boil, cover and reduce heat. Simmer for 30 minutes.
3. Remove the bay leaves. Liquidize soup. Return to pan, season to taste, reheat and serve garnished with the finely chopped chives or parsley.

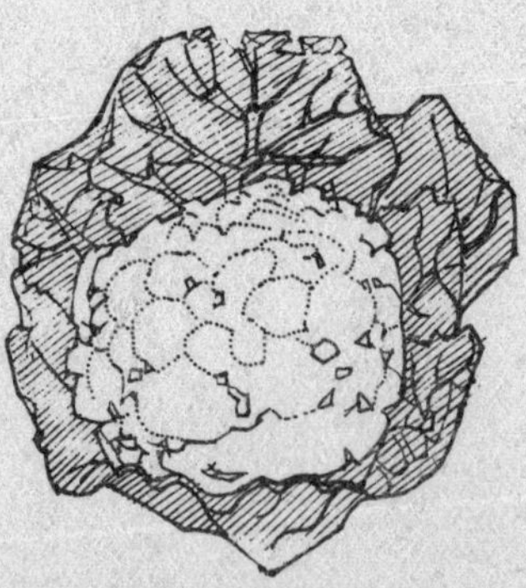

CELERY AND CARROT SOUP

Serves 5. Supplies 2.5g protein/90 calories per portion.

Imperial (Metric)	American
1 small onion	1 small onion
1 head of celery	1 head of celery
3 large carrots	3 large carrots
1 oz (25g) soft vegetable margarine or butter	2½ tablespoonsful soft vegetable margarine or butter
1 oz (25g) wholemeal flour	¼ cupful wholewheat flour
2 pints (1 litre) vegetable stock	5 cupsful vegetable stock
3 large tomatoes, tinned or fresh	3 large tomatoes canned or fresh
Bay leaf	Bay leaf
Pinch nutmeg	Pinch nutmeg
Sea salt	Sea salt
Freshly ground black pepper	Freshly ground black pepper
2 tablespoonsful top of the milk	2 tablespoonsful top of the milk

1. Finely chop the onion, celery and carrots and cook together in the margarine or butter over a low heat for a couple of minutes.
2. Stir in the flour and then gradually add the stock and tomatoes (skinned if using fresh). Add the bay leaf and bring to the boil, then reduce heat and simmer for 30 minutes. Remove the bayleaf.
3. Liquidize and then reheat adding the pinch of nutmeg and seasoning to taste. Serve with a little top of the milk swirled into each bowl.

CUCUMBER SOUP

Serves 4. Supplies 1g protein/100 calories per portion.

A delicate chilled soup with cream cheese to give a smooth texture.

Imperial (Metric)	American
1 small onion	1 small onion
1 cucumber	1 cucumber
4 teaspoonsful chopped mint	4 teaspoonsful chopped mint
1½ pints (¾ litre) vegetable stock	3¾ cupsful vegetable stock
3 oz (75g) cream cheese	⅓ cupful cream cheese
1 teaspoonful cornflour	1 teaspoonful cornflour
Sea salt	Sea salt
Freshly ground black pepper	Freshly ground black pepper

1. Chop the onion and cucumber, reserving a 2 oz (50g) chunk of cucumber for garnish.
2. Place half the mint and the chopped onion and cucumber with the stock in a pan and bring to the boil. Then reduce heat and simmer for 20 minutes until the vegetables are soft. Strain.
3. Blend the cornflour with the cream cheese, add a little of the soup liquid to form a smooth paste. Then stir this mixture into the soup.
4. Bring to the boil, stirring well, and cook for 2 minutes, until it thickens slightly. Remove from heat, season to taste and chill for 2 hours.
5. Just before serving chop the remaining cucumber and sprinkle on top of soup with the remaining mint.

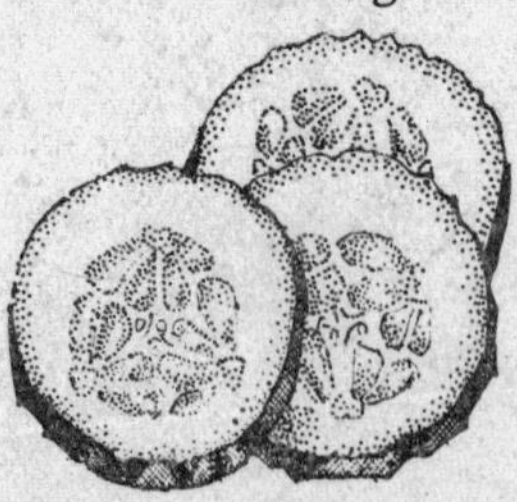

FRENCH ONION SOUP

Serves 4. Supplies 1.5g protein/130 calories per portion.

Imperial (Metric)
1 lb (½ kilo) onions
2 oz (50g) butter
1 tablespoonful wholemeal flour
2 pints (1 litre) vegetable stock
Bay leaf
Pinch dried rosemary
Freshly ground black pepper

American
1 pound onions
¼ cupful butter
1 tablespoonful wholewheat flour
5 cupsful vegetable stock
Bay leaf
Pinch dried rosemary
Freshly ground black pepper

1. Very finely chop the onions. Cook over a low heat in the butter for 10 minutes, until they turn a golden colour.
2. Stir in the flour and cook for 1 minute and then add the stock, bay leaf and rosemary. Bring to the boil, then reduce heat, cover and simmer for 20 minutes. Remove bay leaf, season with pepper and serve.

LENTIL SOUP

Serves 4. Supplies 6.3g protein/108 calories per portion.

A substantial soup with a hearty texture and warm colour.

Imperial (Metric)
1 large onion
1 large carrot
1 dessertspoonful vegetable oil
4 oz (100g) red lentils
1½ pints (¾ litre) water or vegetable stock
2 bay leaves
Sea salt
Freshly ground black pepper

American
1 large onion
1 large carrot
2 teaspoonsful vegetable oil
½ cupful red lentils
3¾ cupsful water or vegetable stock
2 bay leaves
Sea salt
Freshly ground black pepper

1. Chop the onion and finely dice the carrot. *Sauté* together in the oil for 2 minutes.
2. Add the lentils, water or stock, and bay leaves. Bring to the boil. Reduce heat, cover and simmer for 30 minutes until the lentils and vegetables are quite soft.
3. Remove the bay leaves, liquidize the soup and then reheat. Season to taste and serve.

MINESTRONE

Serves 4. Supplies 3.5g protein/90 calories per portion.

A warming soup, ideal for cold winter days.

Imperial (Metric)	**American**
1 large onion	1 large onion
2 sticks celery	2 stalks celery
1 large carrot	1 large carrot
1 large potato	1 large potato
4 oz (100g) white cabbage	4 ounces white cabbage
1 clove garlic	1 clove garlic
1 dessertspoonful olive oil	2 teaspoonsful olive oil
3 large tomatoes, tinned or fresh	3 large tomatoes, canned of fresh
Pinch dried sage	Pinch dried sage
½ teaspoonful oregano	½ teaspoonful oregano
2 bay leaves	2 bay leaves
2 pints (1 litre) stock or water	5 cupsful stock or water
1 oz (25g) wholemeal spaghetti broken into short lengths	1 ounce wholewheat spaghetti, broken into short lengths
2 oz (50g) frozen peas (optional)	2½ tablespoonsful frozen peas (optional)
Sea salt	Sea salt
Freshly ground black pepper	Freshly ground black pepper

1. Finely chop the onion and celery. Scrub the carrot and dice finely. Peel and finely dice the potato. Finely shred the cabbage and crush the garlic clove.
2. Heat the oil and *sauté* together all the vegetables for 2 minutes.
3. Add the tomatoes (skinned and chopped if using fresh), the herbs and stock or water. Bring to the boil, then cover, reduce heat and simmer for 30 minutes. Add spaghetti and cook 5 minutes. Finally, add the peas and cook for a further 5 minutes. Season to taste, and serve.

MUSHROOM SOUP

Serves 4. Supplies 3.8g protein/140 calories per portion.

Imperial (Metric)
1 large onion
1 medium potato
½ lb (¼ kilo) button mushrooms
1½ oz (40g) butter or soft vegetable margarine
½ pint (¼ litre) skimmed milk
¾ pint (400ml) water or vegetable stock
1 teaspoonful thyme
Sea salt
Freshly ground black pepper
Parsley to garnish

American
1 large onion
1 medium potato
4 cupsful button mushrooms
3½ tablespoonsful butter or soft vegetable margarine
1½ cupsful skimmed milk
2 cupsful water or vegetable stock
1 teaspoonful thyme
Sea salt
Freshly ground black pepper
Parsley to garnish

1. Chop the onion, dice the potato and slice the mushrooms.
2. Cook together for 3 minutes in the fat. Stir in the milk and water or stock and the thyme. Bring to the boil, then reduce heat, cover and simmer for 20 minutes.
3. Liquidize, reheat and season to heat. Garnish with some chopped parsley.

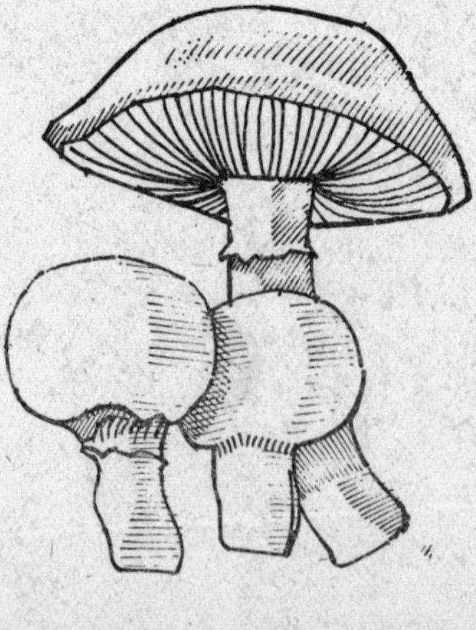

SPROUT AND POTATO SOUP

Serves 4. Supplies 4.4g protein/120 calories per portion.

Imperial (Metric)	**American**
½ lb (¼ kilo) Brussels sprouts	8 ounces Brussels sprouts
½ lb (¼ kilo) potato	8 ounces potato
1 small leek	1 small leek
1 tablespoonful oil	1 tablespoonful oil
1¼ pints (650ml) vegetable stock	3¼ cupsful vegetable stock
¼ pint (150ml) milk	⅔ cupful milk
Sea salt	Sea salt
Freshly ground black pepper	Freshly ground black pepper

1. Remove discoloured outer leaves from the sprouts, wash and roughly chop.
2. Peel and dice the potato. Trim, wash and chop the leek.
3. Cook all together in the oil over a low heat for 2 minutes and then add the stock. Bring to the boil, then reduce heat and simmer for 20 minutes until the vegetables are soft.
4. Liquidize the soup. Reheat, adding the milk and seasoning to taste.

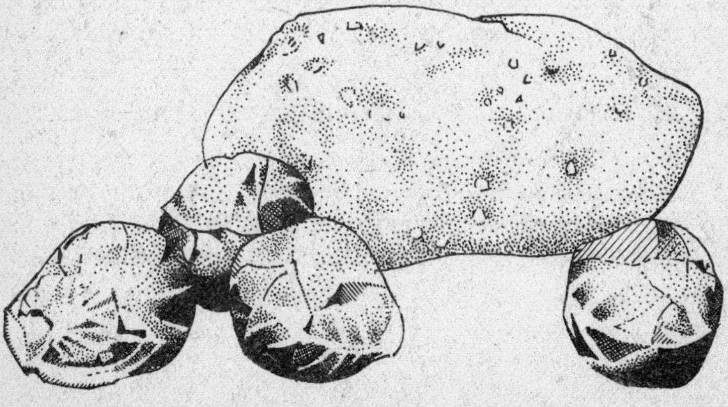

SWEETCORN CHOWDER

Serves 4. Supplies 8g protein/240 calories per portion.

Served with warm wholemeal bread, a complete main course.

Imperial (Metric)	American
1 large onion	1 large onion
½ lb (¼ kilo) potato	8 ounces potato
1 green pepper	1 green pepper
1 stick celery	1 stalk celery
1 tablespoonful oil	1 tablespoonful oil
1 bay leaf	1 bay leaf
1 pint (½ litre) vegetable stock or water	2½ cupsful vegetable stock or water
1 tablespoonful cornflour	1 tablespoonful cornflour
¾ pint (400ml) milk	2 cupsful milk
¾ lb (300g) sweetcorn kernels	2 cupsful sweetcorn kernels
Sea salt	Sea salt
Freshly ground black pepper	Freshly ground black pepper
Finely chopped parsley	Finely chopped parsley

1. Finely chop the onion, peel and dice the potato, dice the pepper and finely chop the celery. Cook together over a low heat in the oil for a few minutes.
2. Add the bay leaf and the stock or water. Bring to the boil, then reduce heat to a simmer and cook for 20 minutes, until the potato is soft.
3. Mix the cornflour to a smooth paste with a little of the milk.
4. Stir paste into the soup with the rest of the milk and the sweetcorn. Stir continually as it comes to the boil, then cook for 2 minutes to let the cornflour thicken the soup. Season to taste and reduce heat to a simmer cook for 5 minutes. Garnish with parsley.

VEGETABLE MEDLEY SOUP

Serves 5. Supplies 4g protein/120 calories per serving.

Imperial (Metric)	**American**
3 leeks	3 leeks
1 turnip	1 turnip
3 carrots	3 carrots
1 medium potato	1 medium potato
1 tablespoonful oil	1 tablespoonful oil
1 oz (25g) red lentils	2½ tablespoonsful red lentils
2 pints (1 litre) water	5 cupsful water
2 bay leaves	2 bay leaves
¼ pint (150ml) milk	⅔ cupful milk
Sea salt	Sea salt
Freshly ground black pepper	Freshly ground black pepper

1. Trim the leeks and slice lengthwise through the centre, wash thoroughly and then slice finely. Peel and dice the turnip; scrub and dice the carrot and the potato.
2. Place the oil in the pan and add the vegetables. Stir in well and cook over a low heat for 5 minutes.
3. Add the lentils, water and bay leaves and bring to the boil. Reduce heat, cover and simmer for 40 minutes. Remove bay leaves.
4. Liquidize soup and then return to pan. Stir in milk and season to taste. Reheat and serve.

VICHYSSOISE

Serves 4. Supplies 4g protein/160 calories per portion — with cream supplies 4.09g protein/240 calories per portion.

A classic soup — cut down on the protein and calories by omitting the cream. Traditionally served chilled, but it is equally tasty served hot as a warming light lunch — complete with a wholemeal roll.

Imperial (Metric)	**American**
2 large leeks	2 large leeks
1 large onion	1 large onion
1 tablespoonful vegetable oil	1 tablespoonful vegetable oil
4 medium potatoes	4 medium potatoes
1½ pints (¾ litre) water or vegetable stock	3¾ cupsful water or vegetable stock
Bay leaf	Bay leaf
Sea salt	Sea salt
Freshly ground black pepper	Freshly ground black pepper
¼ pint (150ml) single cream (optional)	⅔ cupful light cream (optional)

1. Trim the leeks to within 1 in. (2cm) of the white stem and cut off the roots. Slice lengthwise, cut into chunks and wash thoroughly.
2. Finely chop the onion and peel and dice the potato. *Sauté* together with the chopped leeks in the oil over a low heat for 2 minutes.
3. Add the stock and bay leaf. Bring to the boil, then reduce heat, simmer for 35 minutes until the vegetables are quite tender.
4. Remove the bay leaf, liquidize and season to taste and stir in the cream if using. Then chill for 2 hours — or reheat and serve hot.

WATERCRESS SOUP

Serve 4. Supplies 3g protein/120 calories per portion.

An attractive pale green in colour, this soup makes the most of mineral-rich watercress.

Imperial (Metric)	American
1 bunch watercress	1 bunch watercress
1 lb (1/2 kilo) potatoes	1 pound potatoes
1 large onion	1 large onion
1 dessertspoonful vegetable oil	2 teaspoonsful vegetable oil
1 1/4 pints (650ml) water	3 1/4 cupsful water
Sea salt	Sea salt
Freshly ground black pepper	Freshly ground black pepper

1. Wash and roughly chop the watercress, reserving a few leaves for garnish.
2. Scrub and dice the potatoes and roughly chop the onion. *Sauté* these together in the oil for 2 minutes.
3. Stir in the watercress and the water, bring to the boil, cover and reduce heat. Simmer for 20 minutes.
4. Liquidize soup and reheat, season to taste, garnish and serve.

WHOLEMEAL CROISSANTS

Makes 24 croissants. 3.5g protein/150 calories each.

Serve wholemeal croissants with soup as a special treat — higher in fat than standard wholemeal bread, so not ideal for everyday consumption. But their light texture and buttery flavour make these irresistable. They are also surprisingly easy to make and are lovely for breakfast too.

Imperial (Metric)
1 oz (25g) fresh yeast
½ pint (¼ litre) tepid milk
4 fl oz (120ml) tepid water
1 teaspoonful honey
2 oz (50g) butter or soft vegetable margarine, melted and cooled
20 oz (550g) wholemeal flour
1 teaspoonful sea salt
6 oz (150g) butter
Top of the milk

American
2½ tablespoonsful fresh yeast
1⅓ cupsful tepid milk
⅔ cupful tepid water
1 teaspoonful honey
5 tablespoonsful butter or soft vegetable margarine, melted and cooled
5 cupsful wholewheat flour
1 teaspoonful sea salt
⅔ cupful butter
Top of the milk

1. Crumble the yeast into a jug and mix in the tepid milk and water. Stir in the honey and the melted and cooled butter or margarine. Leave to stand for 5 minutes.
2. Rub the remaining butter into the flour and salt until the mixture resembles fine breadcrumbs.
3. Make a well in centre and pour in the yeast liquid, mixing in thoroughly to form a wet dough. Cover and leave to stand until doubled in size. The mixture is now ready to use.
4. Divide the dough into three. Roll each third into a circle about 10 in. (25cm) across. Cut into eight equal segments and roll up gently into a crescent shape, from the longer side, moistening the tip with a little water to stick.

5. Transfer to a lightly greased baking tray and leave to prove for 20 minutes in a warm place until double in size.

6. Brush gently with top of the milk and bake at 425°F/220°C (Gas Mark 7) for 25 minutes until golden brown.

Note: If liked the dough can be divided into three and one or two thirds can be kept in the refrigerator for up to two days.

6.
MAIN COURSES

CAULIFLOWER SURPRISE

Serves 4. Supplies 10g protein/350 calories per portion.

Imperial (Metric)	American
1 large cauliflower or 2 small ones	1 large cauliflower or 2 small ones
1 large onion	1 large onion
6 oz (150g) sweetcorn kernels	1 cupful sweetcorn kernels
6 oz (150g) courgettes	2 zucchini
4 oz (100g) mushrooms	2 cupsful mushrooms
½ green pepper	½ green pepper
1 oz (25g) soft vegetable margarine	2½ tablespoonsful soft vegetable margarine
1 oz (25g) wholemeal flour	¼ cupful wholewheat flour
¼ pint (150ml) skimmed milk	⅔ cupful skimmed milk
About ¼ pint (150ml) stock from cauliflower	About ⅔ cupful stock from cauliflower
Sea salt	Sea salt
Freshly ground black pepper	Freshly ground black pepper
1 oz (25g) Cheddar cheese	¼ cupful Cheddar cheese
2 tablespoonsful sesame seeds	2 tablespoonsful sesame seeds

1. Divide cauliflower into large florets and place in a pan with 1 in. (2cm) boiling water. Cover and cook for 8 minutes. Drain, reserving cooking water.

2. Finely chop the onion. If using fresh sweetcorn cook for a few minutes until just soft. Slice courgettes (zucchini) into ½ in. (1cm) slices and plunge into a little boiling water and cook for 2 minutes. Finely slice the mushrooms and pepper.
3. Melt margarine in pan and cook onion for 2 minutes. Stir in the flour and cook for a minute, stirring constantly. Gradually add the milk and stock, beating to prevent lumps forming. Bring to the boil and cook for 1 minute.
4. Reduce heat and stir in the sweetcorn, courgettes (zucchini), mushrooms, pepper and season lightly. Stir in well and cook for 3 minutes.
5. Grate the cheese. Place cauliflower florets in a deep pie dish. Pour sauce over, coating all the cauliflower.
6. Sprinkle cheese and sesame seeds on top and grill for a few minutes until the topping is crunchy and golden.

CAULIFLOWER CUSTARD

Serves 4. Supplies 13g protein/200 calories per portion.

Imperial (Metric)	**American**
1 large cauliflower	1 large cauliflower
2 bay leaves	2 bay leaves
1 onion	1 onion
2 tablespoonsful tomato *purée*	2 tablespoonsful tomato paste
1 tablespoonful vegetable oil	1 tablespoonful vegetable oil
4 eggs	4 eggs
¼ pint (150ml) skimmed milk	⅔ cupful skimmed milk
Parsley	Parsley
1 oz (25g) grated Cheddar cheese	¼ cupful grated Cheddar cheese
Sea salt	Sea salt
Freshly ground black pepper	Freshly ground black pepper

1. Divide cauliflower into florets and place in pan with bay leaves with ½ in. (1cm) boiling water. Cover and cook for 10 minutes.
2. Finely chop the onion and *sauté* in the oil for 2 minutes.
3. Stir in the tomato *purée* and cook for 2 minutes.
4. Drain cauliflower and place in an 8 in. (20cm) pie plate, sprinkle with onion and tomato mixture.
5. Beat eggs with the milk and stir in 2 tablespoonsful finely chopped parsley pour over the cauliflower, top with the cheese and bake for 30 minutes in a pre-heated oven 400°F/200°C (Gas Mark 6) until well risen and golden. Serve with a green vegetable or a crunchy winter salad.

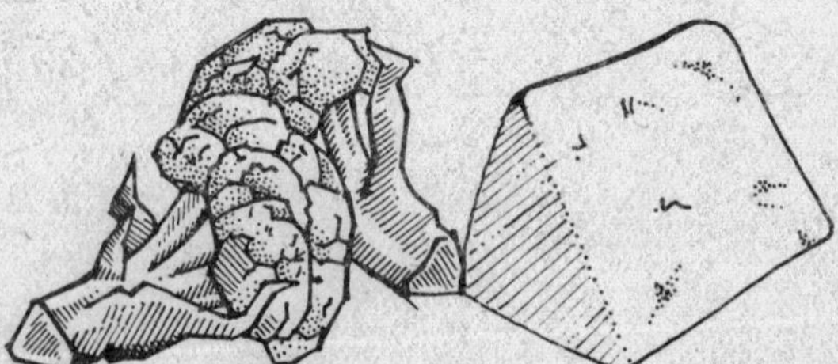

MEATLESS MOUSSAKA

Serves 4. Supplies 8g protein/230 calories per portion.

Imperial (Metric)
2 large aubergines
2 tablespoonsful olive oil
½ oz (15g) soft vegetable margarine
½ oz (15g) wholemeal flour
¼ pint (150ml) skimmed milk
2 oz (50g) strong Cheddar cheese
Sea salt
Freshly ground black pepper
Tomato Sauce (page 68)

American
2 large eggplants
2 tablespoonsful olive oil
1 tablespoonful soft vegetable margarine
2 tablespoonsful wholewheat flour
⅔ cupful skimmed milk
½ cupful strong Cheddar cheese
Sea salt
Freshly ground black pepper
Tomato Sauce (page 68)

1. Cut the aubergines (eggplants) into slices ¼ in. (½cm) thick, sprinkle with a little salt and leave for 30 minutes to draw out the bitterness.
2. Melt the margarine in a pan. Stir in the flour and gradually add the milk, stirring constantly. Bring to the boil and then reduce heat.
3. Grate the cheese and stir it into the sauce. Season. Remove from heat till required.
4. Pat dry the aubergine (eggplant) slices and lightly fry in the oil till golden. Place a layer in the base of a deep ovenproof dish. Top with a layer of tomato sauce, then add another layer of aubergine (eggplant). Repeat till all used up — then pour on the cheese sauce, cover with foil and bake for 40 minutes at 375°F/190°C (Gas Mark 5). Serve with a lightly cooked green vegetable, or a green salad.

DOLMADES

Serves 4. Supplies 5g protein/215 calories per portion.

Imperial (Metric)	American
1 large savoy cabbage or 12 vine leaves	1 large savoy cabbage or 12 vine leaves
1 medium-sized aubergine	1 medium-sized eggplant
Sea salt	Sea salt
1 large onion	1 large onion
2 cloves garlic	2 cloves garlic
1 tablespoonful oil	1 tablespoonful oil
6 oz (150g) long-grain brown rice	¾ cupful long-grain brown rice
¼ pint (150ml) white wine	⅔ cupful white wine
¼ pint (150ml) water	⅔ cupful water
3 fresh tomatoes or 1 small tin	3 fresh tomatoes or 1 small can
1 green pepper	1 green pepper
Pinch oregano	Pinch oregano
1 tablespoonful chopped parsley	1 tablespoonful chopped parsley
Freshly ground black pepper	Freshly ground black pepper
A little extra water or stock	A little extra water or stock

1. Cut the aubergine (eggplant) into ¼ in. (½cm) thick slices, sprinkle with salt and leave for 30 minutes. Pat dry and dice.
2. Finely chop the onion and crush the garlic. Cook together for few minutes in the oil without browning.
3. Stir in the rice and cook for 2 minutes. Stir in the wine and water and add the tomatoes (skinned and chopped if using fresh). Bring to the boil, reduce heat, cover and simmer. Finely chop the pepper and stir into the rice mixture with the herbs. Cook for a further 20 minutes, until rice is just soft and liquid absorbed.
4. While rice is cooking.prepare the leaves. Remove tough outer leaves from the cabbage. Carefully take 12 leaves and plunge into boiling water for 2 minutes. Drain. (Vine leaves don't need blanching.)

5. Divide cooked filling between the leaves, placing a little in the centre of each leaf across the width. Carefully roll up. Place in a shallow ovenproof dish making sure the leaf join is underneath. Pour over a little water to moisten, cover with foil and cook for 20 minutes at 375°F/190°C (Gas Mark 5). Serve with a fresh tomato sauce (page 68), a green salad and a little crusty bread to complete the protein.

STUFFED AUBERGINES

Serves 4. Supplies 8g protein/180 calories per portion.

Imperial (Metric)	**American**
2 medium aubergines	2 medium eggplants
1 large onion	1 large onion
½ lb (¼ kilo) mushrooms	4 cupsful mushrooms
1 tablespoonful oil	1 tablespoonful oil
3 oz (75g) wholemeal breadcrumbs	1½ cupsful wholewheat breadcrumbs
2 tablespoonsful tomato *purée*	2 tablespoonsful tomato paste
3 oz (75g) Cheddar cheese, grated	¾ cupful Cheddar cheese, grated
2 tablespoonsful chopped parsley	2 tablespoonsful chopped parsley
Sea salt	Sea salt
Freshly ground black pepper	Freshly ground black pepper

1. Place the aubergines (eggplants) in boiling water and simmer for 5 minutes.
2. Finely chop the onion and slice the mushrooms and cook in the oil for a few minutes. Stir in the breadcrumbs, tomato *purée*, cheese and parsley. Cook for a further 2 minutes. Remove from heat.
3. Cut the aubergines (eggplants) in half lengthwise and scoop out most of the flesh, leaving a thin but firm shell. Chop flesh roughly and stir into cheese mixture. Season to taste.
4. Place the skins on a lightly greased ovenproof dish and divide the filling between them, stuffing in firmly.
5. Cover with foil and cook for 30 minutes at 375°F/190°C (Gas Mark 5). Remove foil and cook for a further 10 minutes. Serve with crispy roast potatoes and a green salad.

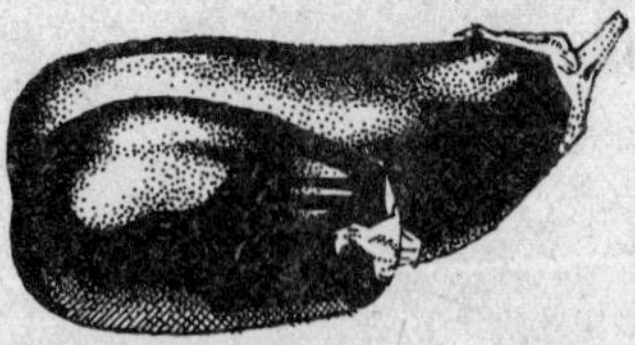

AUBERGINE AND CHICK PEA PÂTÉ

Serves 5. Supplies 5g protein/90 calories per portion.

Based on the traditional Middle Eastern dish, *hummus*. Aubergines (eggplants) are added to lower the protein content — the peas, yogurt and tahini (sesame seed paste) make a balanced protein dish. Serve with thinly cut crudités of raw vegetables for a substantial lunch or light supper dish.

Imperial (Metric)	**American**
4 oz (100g) chick peas, soaked overnight	½ cupful garbanzo beans, soaked overnight
1 large aubergine	1 large eggplant
A smear of oil	A smear of oil
1 tablespoonful tahini	1 tablespoonful tahini
1 tablespoonful yogurt	1 tablespoonful yogurt
Juice of 2 lemons	Juice of 2 lemons
3 cloves garlic	3 cloves garlic
Sea salt	Sea salt
Freshly ground black pepper	Freshly ground black pepper
Chopped parsley to garnish	Chopped parsley to garnish

1. Drain the chick peas (garbanzo beans) and cook in fresh water until soft.
2. While cooking, prepare the aubergine (eggplant). Rub the oil into the skin place on a piece of foil and bake for 1 hour at 375°F/190°C (Gas Mark 5). Remove from oven and scoop out flesh from skin.
3. Place the drained, cooked chick peas (garbanzo beans) in liquidizer with the aubergine (eggplant), tahini, yogurt, lemon juice, crushed cloves of garlic and a little seasoning. Blend until smooth. Turn out and pile into a dish. Sprinkle parsley over top.

STIR-FRY VEGETABLES

Serves 4. Supplies 7g protein/60 calories per portion.

The Oriental technique of quickly cooking vegetables in a wok helps to retain nutritional value. The variations are almost endless. Here is a basic recipe — add different vegetables of your choice.

Imperial (Metric)	**American**
1 leek	1 leek
½ small savoy cabbage	½ small savoy cabbage
1 green pepper	1 green pepper
1 red pepper	1 red pepper
2 large carrots	2 large carrots
1 small swede	1 small rutabaga
1 tablespoonful oil	1 tablespoonful oil
2 tablespoonsful soya sauce	2½ tablespoonsful soy sauce
¼ pint (150ml) water	⅔ cupful water
1 tablespoonful dry sherry	1 tablespoonful dry sherry
Pinch sea salt	Pinch sea salt
Freshly ground black pepper	Freshly ground black pepper
2 handfuls beansprouts	2 handfuls beansprouts
3 oz (75g) cashew nuts	⅔ cupful cashew nuts

1. Prepare the vegetables. Remove the tough green top from the leek and cut off the roots. Slice into fine rings. Finely shred the cabbage, cut the peppers into fine strips about 2 in. (5cm) long, scrub the carrots and cut into thin strips, peel and do the same for the swede (rutabaga).
2. Heat the oil in a wok or large heavy-based frying pan (skillet). Add the prepared vegetables and stir around well so all are coated and cook for 2 minutes.
3. Mix together the soya sauce, water and sherry and season lightly. Pour over the vegetables and continue cooking for a further 2 minutes. Add the beansprouts and stir in well. Cook for 1 minute and then add the cashew nuts. Stir around well and serve immediately with rice to complement the protein.

MUSHROOM TARTLETS

Makes 4. Each supplies 11g protein/360 calories.

Pastry:

Imperial (Metric)	**American**
3 oz (75g) soft vegetable margarine	1/3 cupful soft vegetable margarine
6 oz (150g) wholemeal flour	1 1/2 cupsful wholewheat flour
Pinch sea salt	Pinch sea salt
Cold water to mix	Cold water to mix

Filling:

Imperial (Metric)	**American**
1/2 lb (1/4 kilo) button mushrooms	4 cupsful button mushrooms
1 small onion	1 small onion
1 clove garlic	1 clove garlic
1 dessertspoonful oil	2 teaspoonsful oil
2 eggs	2 eggs
1/4 pint (150ml) natural yogurt	2/3 cupful natural yogurt
1 tablespoonful finely chopped chives or parsley	1 tablespoonful finely chopped chives or parsley

1. Rub the margarine into the flour and salt. Add sufficient water to bind to a soft dough and roll out and line four small tartlet tins. Bake blind for 10 minutes at 400°F/200°C (Gas Mark 6).

2. Meanwhile prepare the filling. Finely chop the mushrooms and onion, and crush the garlic. Cook gently together in the oil for 3 minutes.

3. Place in the part-baked flan cases. Beat together the eggs and yogurt and chives, season lightly and pour into the flan cases. Return to oven and cook for a further 20 minutes until the filling is firm to the touch.

VEGETABLE PASTIES

Makes 4 pasties. Supplies 11g protein/380 calories each.

Pastry:

Imperial (Metric)	American
3 oz (75g) soft vegetable margarine	1/3 cupful soft vegetable margarine
6 oz (150g) wholemeal flour	1 1/2 cupsful wholewheat flour
Pinch sea salt	Pinch sea salt
Cold water to mix	Cold water to mix

Filling:

Imperial (Metric)	American
1 small onion	1 small onion
A few strips of green pepper	A few strips of green pepper
1 oz (25g) mushrooms	1/2 cupful mushrooms
A smear of oil	A smear of oil
10 oz (300g) mixed root vegetables, finely diced	10 ounces root vegetables, finely diced
3 oz (75g) grated cheese	3/4 cupful grated cheese
A few sprigs fresh rosemary or 1/2 teaspoonful dried	A few sprigs fresh rosemary or 1/2 teaspoonful dried
Sea salt	Sea salt
Freshly ground black pepper	Freshly ground black pepper

1. Rub the margarine into the flour and salt, until the mixture resembles fine breadcrumbs. Add sufficient cold water to mix to a soft dough. Roll out to a large oval shape and cut out 4 circles, 7 in. (18cm) diameter.
2. Finely chop the onion, pepper and mushrooms and cook gently in the oil for 2 minutes. Mix with other prepared vegetables and stir in the cheese, rosemary and seasoning.
3. Divide the filling between the pasties and place across the centre of each circle.

4. Brush lightly with water around the edge of the circle and then draw up both sides, to meet in the centre above the filling. Pinch together and flute with the back of a knife.

5. Lightly glaze with a little milk and bake at 400°F/200°C (Gas Mark 6) for 15 minutes and then at 350°F/180°C (Gas Mark 4) for a further 10 minutes. Serve hot with a baked potato and salad, or cold as a packed lunch.

CREAMY ASPARAGUS FLAN

Serves 4. Supplies 7g protein/280 calories per portion.

Pastry:

Imperial (Metric)	**American**
2 oz (50g) soft vegetable margarine	1/4 cupful soft vegetable margarine
4 oz (100g) wholemeal flour	1 cupful wholewheat flour
Pinch sea salt	Pinch sea salt

Filling:

Imperial (Metric)	**American**
3/4 lb (350g) asparagus tips	12 ounces asparagus tips
1/4 pint (150ml) single cream	2/3 cupful light cream
1 egg	1 egg
Sea salt	Sea salt
Freshly ground black pepper	Freshly ground black pepper

1. Rub margarine into flour and salt until mixture resembles fine breadcrumbs. Add sufficient cold water to mix to a soft dough. Roll out to line a 7 in. (18cm) flan dish and bake blind for 10 minutes at 400°F/200°C (Gas Mark 6).

2. Steam the asparagus until just tender. Arrange in flan case with tips radiating out from centre.

3. Beat egg with cream and season lightly. Pour into flan case and bake for 25 minutes at 375°F/190°C (Gas Mark 5) until filling is firm.

SPINACH TART

Serves 5. Supplies 10g protein/250 calories per portion.

Pastry:

Imperial (Metric)	American
3 oz (75g) soft vegetable margarine	1/3 cupful soft vegetable margarine
6 oz (150g) wholemeal flour	1½ cupsful wholewheat flour
Sea salt	Sea salt
Cold water to mix	Cold water to mix

Filling:

Imperial (Metric)	American
¾ lb (350g) frozen spinach or 1 lb (½ kilo) fresh	12 ounces frozen spinach or 1 pound fresh
1 small onion	1 small onion
½ green pepper	½ green pepper
1 dessertspoonful vegetable oil	2 teaspoonsful vegetable oil
Pinch nutmeg	Pinch nutmeg
¼ pint (150ml) natural yogurt	2/3 cupful natural yogurt
2 eggs	2 eggs
Sea salt	Sea salt
Freshly ground black pepper	Freshly ground black pepper

1. Rub margarine into flour, add a pinch of salt. Refrigerate while preparing the filling.
2. If using frozen spinach thaw out, and drain well. If using fresh, wash well, place leaves in pan, cover and cook with no extra water over a low heat for a couple of minutes until soft. Drain and cut up finely.
3. Finely chop the onion and pepper, cook gently in the oil for 2 minutes. Remove from heat and in a bowl mix with the spinach and nutmeg. Beat the eggs with the yogurt and season.

4. Add sufficient cold water to the flour mix to form a dough. Roll out lightly and line an 8 in. (20cm) flan dish. Bake blind for 10 minutes, at 400°F/200°C (Gas Mark 6).

5. Place spinach in flan dish, pour over eggs and yogurt mixture, and return to oven and cook for 30 minutes until set and well risen.

MUSHROOM TOPPED SPAGHETTI

Serves 4. Supplies 12g protein/300 calories per portion.

Imperial (Metric)	**American**
2 large onions	2 large onions
2 cloves garlic	2 cloves garlic
2 tablespoonsful olive oil	2 tablespoonsful olive oil
10 large open mushrooms	10 large open mushrooms
15 oz (425g) tin or	1 medium can or
1 lb (½ kilo) fresh tomatoes	1 pound fresh tomatoes
1 red pepper	1 red pepper
1 teaspoonful basil	1 teaspoonful basil
1 teaspoonful oregano	1 teaspoonful oregano
Sea salt	Sea salt
Freshly ground black pepper	Freshly ground black pepper
½ lb (¼ kilo) wholemeal spaghetti	8 ounces wholewheat spaghetti

1. Finely chop the onion and garlic. Cook together in the oil for a few minutes.

2. Wipe and slice the mushrooms and stir into the pan. Add the tomatoes (skinned and chopped if using fresh). Finely chop the pepper and add to the pan with the herbs. Bring to the boil, then reduce heat and simmer for 40 minutes, stirring occasionally.

3. 15 minutes before the end of cooking time, put the spaghetti into boiling salted water.

4. If sauce is still too liquid at the end of cooking, turn up heat and cook uncovered fiercely for a few minutes to reduce the sauce. Divide spaghetti between four plates and pour sauce over.

LEEK QUICHE

Serves 4. Supplies 12g protein/280 calories per portion.

Pastry:

Imperial (Metric)	American
2 oz (50g) soft vegetable margarine	¼ cupful soft vegetable margarine
4 oz (100g) wholemeal flour	1 cupful wholewheat flour
Pinch sea salt	Pinch sea salt
4 teaspoonsful cold water	4 teaspoonsful cold water

Filling:

Imperial (Metric)	American
3 leeks	3 leeks
2 eggs	2 eggs
¼ pint (150ml) yogurt	⅔ cupful yogurt
1 oz (25g) Cheddar	¼ cupful Cheddar
Pinch dried rosemary	Pinch dried rosemary
Sea salt	Sea salt
Freshly ground black pepper	Freshly ground black pepper

1. Rub margarine into flour and salt, until mixture resembles fine breadcrumbs. Chill while preparing the filling.
2. Cut the coarse green tops off the leeks. Slice into ¾ in. (2cm) thick slices and wash well. Plunge into boiling water and cook for 5 minutes. Drain well.
3. Beat the eggs with the yogurt. Grate the cheese.
4. Add water to the pastry mix to form a soft dough. Roll out to line a 7 in. (18cm) flan dish. Arrange the leeks in the dish. Pour over the egg and yogurt mixture, season, add rosemary and sprinkle with cheese. Cook in a pre-heated oven 400°F/200°C (Gas Mark 6) for 30 minutes until the filling is set and the topping golden brown.

COURGETTE BAKE

Serves 4. Supplies 14g protein/290 calories per portion.

A substantial pasta-based dish — a complete main course in itself, simply follow with fresh fruit.

Imperial (Metric)	**American**
6 oz (150g) wholemeal pasta rings	1½ cupsful wholewheat pasta rings
6 large courgettes	6 large zucchini
6 large tomatoes or a 15 oz (425g) tin	6 large tomatoes or 1 medium can
1 large onion	1 large onion
1 tablespoonful vegetable oil	1 tablespoonful vegetable oil
Basil or oregano, 1 teaspoonful dried or 1 tablespoonful fresh	Basil or oregano, 1 teaspoonful dried or 1 tablespoonful fresh
2 oz (50g) hard cheese	½ cupful hard cheese
2 oz (50g) sunflower seeds	½ cupful sunflower seeds
Sea salt	Sea salt
Freshly ground black pepper	Freshly ground black pepper

1. Cook the pasta in boiling water until just soft, about 12 minutes.
2. Cut the courgettes (zucchini) into slices about ¼ in. (½cm) thick and steam or cook in a little boiling water for 2 minutes.
3. Skin and chop the tomatoes if using fresh. Finely chop the onion and cook in the oil for 2 minutes. Stir in the tomatoes and add basil or oregano, finely chopped if using fresh. Bring to boil, cover and simmer for 5 minutes.
4. Grate the cheese and toast the sunflower seeds under a hot grill until just turning golden.
5. Place a layer of pasta rings in a deep pie dish, cover with a layer of courgettes (zucchini), then a layer of tomato mixture. Repeat and sprinkle cheese and sunflower seeds on top. Bake for 20 minutes at 350°F/180°C (Gas Mark 4).

CREAMY MUSHROOM PLAIT

Serves 4. Supplies 6g protein/155 calories per portion.

Dough:

Imperial (Metric)	American
½ oz (15g) soft vegetable margarine	1 tablespoonful soft vegetable margarine
½ lb (¼ kilo) wholemeal flour	2 cupsful wholewheat flour
Pinch sea salt	Pinch sea salt
½ oz (15g) fresh yeast	1 tablespoonful fresh yeast
¼ pint (150ml) tepid water	⅔ cupful tepid water
25mg vitamin C tablet, crushed	25mg vitamin C tablet crushed

Filling:

Imperial (Metric)	American
6 oz (150g) button mushrooms	3 cupsful button mushrooms
1 tablespoonful oil	1 tablespoonful oil
1 small onion	1 small onion
2 tablespoonsful sour cream	2 tablespoonsful sour cream
½ teaspoonful thyme	½ teaspoonful thyme
Sea salt	Sea salt
Freshly ground black pepper	Freshly ground black pepper
A little milk to glaze	A little milk to glaze

1. Rub the margarine into the flour and salt. Add yeast to the water and add the vitamin C tablet. Stir in thoroughly.
2. Add yeast liquid to flour and mix in thoroughly to form a soft dough. Turn onto lightly-floured board or table and knead for 5 minutes until the dough is soft and smooth. Cover and leave to rest for 10 minutes.
3. While dough is resting, lightly grease a baking tray. Slice the mushrooms and cook in the oil until the juice begins to run.
4. Remove from heat and cool slightly. Stir in the cream and the thyme and season.

5. Roll out the dough to a rectangle about 6 × 12 ins. (15 × 30cm), place on baking tray. Spread the mushroom mixture in the centre.
6. Make even diagonal cuts every 1 in. (2cm) on both sides of the rectangle. Fold in the ends of the dough and plait the strips diagonally across the filling.
7. Cover and leave to prove in a warm place for 20 minutes. Then glaze with a little milk and bake at 400°F/200°C (Gas Mark 6) for 20 minutes until the plait is risen and golden.

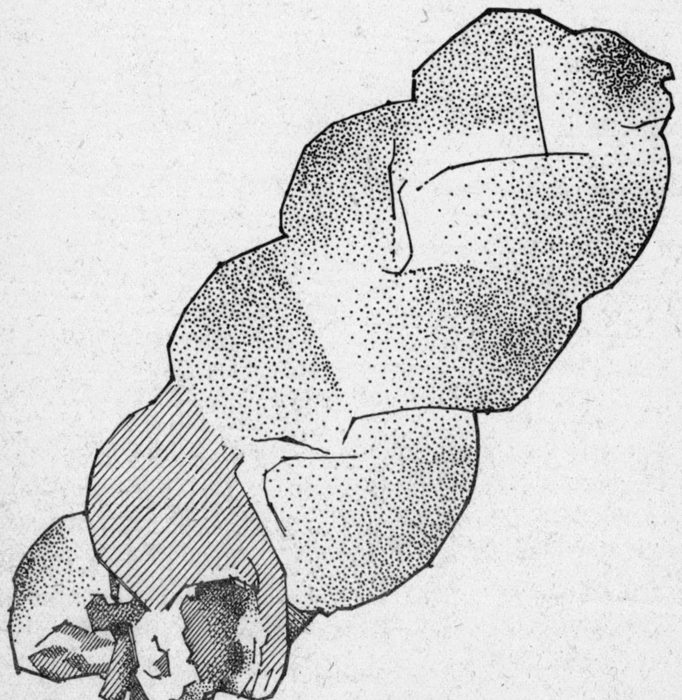

PIZZA

Serves 4 as a main course. Supplies 11g protein/250 calories.

Topping:

Imperial (Metric)	**American**
1 large onion	1 large onion
2 cloves garlic	2 cloves garlic
1 tablespoonful olive oil	1 tablespoonful olive oil
1 teaspoonful oregano	1 teaspoonful oregano
3 large tomatoes	3 large tomatoes
1 green pepper	1 green pepper
4 oz (100g) mushrooms	1 cupful mushrooms
3 oz (75g) Mozzarella cheese, finely sliced	¾ cupful Mozzarella cheese, finely sliced
Sea salt	Sea salt
Freshly ground black pepper	Freshly ground black pepper

Dough:

Imperial (Metric)	**American**
½ oz (15g) soft vegetable margarine	1 tablespoonful soft vegetable margarine
½ lb (¼ kilo) wholemeal flour	2 cupsful wholewheat flour
Pinch sea salt	Pinch sea salt
½ oz (15g) fresh yeast	1 tablespoonful fresh yeast
¼ pint (150ml) tepid water	⅔ cupful tepid water
25mg vitamin C tablet	25mg vitamin C tablet

1. Prepare a tomato sauce for topping. Finely slice the onion, crush the garlic and *sauté* together in the oil for 2 minutes. Add the oregano and the tomatoes, skinned and chopped. Bring to the boil, then reduce heat to a simmer, and cook for 20 minutes.
2. Rub margarine into the flour and salt. Crumble yeast into the water, crush the vitamin C tablet and stir into the liquid. Then add to the flour.

3. Mix in well with your hands, drawing together all the flour. Turn out onto a board or table top and knead for 5 minutes until smooth.
4. Cover with an upturned bowl and leave to rest for 5 minutes. Meanwhile finely chop the pepper and slice the mushrooms.
5. Lightly grease a baking tray. Roll out dough to a circle 9 in. (23cm) in diameter and place on the tray. Spread tomato sauce evenly on top. Sprinkle chopped pepper and mushrooms on top and arrange the cheese slices over them. Season and leave to prove in a warm place for 15 minutes.
6. Bake in a pre-heated oven at 450°F/230°C (Gas Mark 8) for 25 minutes or until the dough is just firm to the touch and the cheese has melted.

SPINACH STUFFED PANCAKES

Serves 4. Sypplies 14g protein/250 calories.

Pancakes:

Imperial (Metric)	**American**
4 oz (100g) wholemeal flour	1 cupful wholewheat flour
Pinch sea salt	Pinch sea salt
2 eggs	2 eggs
¼ pint (150ml) milk	⅔ cupful milk
¼ pint (150ml) water	⅔ cupful water
Oil for frying	Oil for frying

Filling:

Imperial (Metric)	**American**
1 lb (½ kilo) fresh spinach	1 pound fresh spinach
4 oz (100g) Quark	½ cupful Quark
Tomato Sauce (page 68)	Tomato Sauce (page 68)

1. Sieve the flour with the salt. Make a well in the centre and add the eggs. Gradually beat into the flour.

2. Mix together the milk and water and then gradually add half this to the flour, beating it thoroughly. Then continue to beat for 4 minutes.
3. Stir in the remaining liquid. Leave to stand while preparing filling.
4. Remove coarse stems from the spinach. Wash well and place in a pan with no extra water. Cook over a low heat for about 10 minutes until soft. Drain well and chop very finely. Mix into the Quark.
5. Beat the batter again. Smear a small frying pan (skillet) with a little oil. Heat and pour in a little batter, tipping pan to let it spread in a fine coating over the base of the pan.
6. Cook until underside is golden and top is bubbly. Toss or turn pancake over and cook a couple of minutes more. Transfer to a heated plate and keep warm while making the rest of the pancakes.
7. When the pancakes are finished, quickly spread a little filling down the centre of each. Roll up and arrange on plate. Pour sauce over and place in a hot oven 400°F/200°C (Gas Mark 6) for 10 minutes to heat through.

Variations: Fill the pancakes with Stir-Fry Vegetables (page 54), Ratatouille (page 107), or *puréed* aubergines (eggplants) for lower protein fillings.

BRUSSELS MEDLEY

Serves 4. Supplies 13.5g protein/280 calories, per portion.

Cooked vegetables are mixed with wholemeal pasta in a light cheese sauce to give a sustaining macaroni cheese with a difference and a lower protein content too.

Imperial (Metric)	American
½ lb (¼ kilo) Brussels sprouts, cooked	8 ounces Brussels sprouts, cooked
2 carrots, cooked	2 carrots, cooked
6 oz (150g) wholemeal macaroni	1½ cupsful wholewheat macaroni
1 small onion	1 small onion
1 oz (25g) soft vegetable margarine	2½ tablespoonsful soft vegetable margarine
1 oz (25g) wholemeal flour	¼ cupful wholewheat flour
½ pint (300ml) milk	1⅓ cupsful milk
¼ pint (150ml) stock (cooking water from the vegetables)	⅔ cupful stock (cooking water from the vegetables)
2 oz (50g) hard cheese, grated	½ cupful hard cheese, grated
Sea salt	Sea salt
Freshly ground black pepper	Freshly ground black pepper

1. Roughly chop the sprouts and dice the carrots. Cook the macaroni in boiling water for 10 minutes until just soft.
2. Finely chop the onion and cook until soft in the margarine. Stir in the flour and cook for 1 minute. Gradually add the milk and stock stirring constantly and beating to prevent lumps from forming. Bring to the boil and cook for 2 minutes to let it thicken.
3. Stir in half the cheese, reducing heat to a simmer. Stir until the cheese has melted. Add the prepared vegetables and macaroni and stir in thoroughly. Season to taste. Pour into an ovenproof dish and sprinkle the remaining cheese on top. Pop under a hot grill for a few minutes to brown the top.

MUSHROOM LASAGNE

Serves 4. Supplies 11g protein/340 calories per portion.

Imperial (Metric)	American
6 oz (150g) wholemeal lasagne	6 ounces wholewheat lasagne
3 pints (1½ litres) boiling salted water	7½ cupsful boiling salted water

Tomato Sauce:

Imperial (Metric)	American
1 stick celery	1 stalk celery
1 large onion	1 large onion
2 cloves garlic	2 cloves garlic
1 tablespoonful olive oil	1 tablespoonful olive oil
1 green pepper	1 green pepper
6 fresh tomatoes or a 15 oz (425g) tin	6 fresh tomatoes or 1 medium-sized can
1 teaspoonful marjoram	1 teaspoonful marjoram
Sea salt	Sea salt
Freshly ground black pepper	Freshly ground black pepper

Mushroom Sauce:

Imperial (Metric)	American
½ lb (¼ kilo) button mushrooms	4 cupsful button mushrooms
⅓ pint (200ml) skimmed milk	¾ cupful skimmed milk
1 oz (25g) soft vegetable margarine	2½ tablespoonsful soft vegetable margarine
1 oz (25g) wholemeal flour	¼ cupful wholewheat flour

1. Plunge the lasagne into boiling water and cook until just soft — about 12 minutes. Drain, and plunge into cold water. Drain well and set aside.
2. Whilst lasagne is cooking prepare tomato sauce. Chop celery, onion and crush garlic. Cook together in oil for 2 minutes.
3. Chop the pepper. If using fresh tomatoes, skin and chop. Add

pepper and tomatoes to pan with marjoram, stir in well and simmer for 20 minutes. Season to taste.

4. Make mushroom sauce. Cook mushrooms in margarine for 5 minutes. Add flour and stir well. Gradually add the milk, beating in well. Continue stirring until the sauce comes to the boil. Cook for 1 minute and then remove from heat. Season to taste.

5. Lightly grease an oblong ovenproof dish. Place a layer of lasagne in base. Place a layer of tomato sauce on top, then a layer of mushroom sauce. Repeat, using up all ingredients, and finishing with a topping of mushroom sauce. Cover with foil and bake for 40 minutes in a pre-heated oven at 375°F/190°C (Gas Mark 5).

CASHEW ROAST

Serves 4. Supplies 11g protein/290 calories per portion.

Imperial (Metric)	**American**
5 oz (125g) cashew nuts	1 cupful cashew nuts
5 oz (125g) fresh wholemeal breadcrumbs	2½ cupsful fresh wholewheat breadcrumbs
4 oz (100g) mushrooms	2 cupsful mushrooms
1 small onion	1 small onion
Pinch sage	Pinch sage
Pinch dried rosemary	Pinch dried rosemary
Sea salt	Sea salt
Freshly ground black pepper	Freshly ground black pepper
Beaten egg	Beaten egg

1. Grind the nuts and mix with the breadcrumbs. Finely chop the mushrooms and onion. Mix in and add the herbs and season lightly.

2. Add the egg and mix in — moisten with a little extra water if needed.

3. Pile into a greased 1 lb loaf tin, smooth down well and bake at 350°F/180°C (Gas Mark 5) for 50-60 minutes. Turn out and cut into chunky slices. Serve hot or cold, with a salad.

CHESTNUT ROAST

Serves 6. Supplies 6.5g protein/280 calories.

An excellent alternative to Christmas turkey — protein balanced and very tasty.

Imperial (Metric)	American
1 lb (1/2 kilo) chestnuts	1 pound chestnuts
4 sticks celery	4 stalks celery
1 large onion	1 large onion
1 tablespoonful oil	1 tablespoonful oil
6 oz (150g) fresh wholemeal breadcrumbs	3 cupsful fresh wholewheat breadcrumbs
1 handful parsley, finely chopped	1 handful parsley, finely chopped
Pinch dried thyme	Pinch dried thyme
Rind of a lemon	Rind of a lemon
1 egg, beaten	1 egg, beaten
Sea salt	Sea salt
Freshly ground black pepper	Freshly ground black pepper

1. Nick the tops from the chestnuts, place in a pan with cold water. Bring slowly to the boil and then simmer for 20 minutes. While still hot peel them carefully, leaving them in hot water until you're ready to peel them. Finely chop.
2. Finely chop the celery and onion and cook until soft in the oil, without browning.
3. Mix chopped nuts, onion and celery with the breadcrumbs, parsley, thyme, lemon rind. Bind with the beaten egg and season. Place in a lightly greased ring mould and bake for an hour at 350°F/180°C (Gas Mark 4). Turn out and fill centre with Sprouts Purée (page 111).

STUFFED PEPPERS

Serves 4. Supplies 14g protein/355 calories per portion.

Imperial (Metric)	American
6 oz (150g) wholemeal macaroni	1½ cupsful wholewheat macaroni
1 large onion	1 large onion
1 dessertspoonful vegetable oil	2 teaspoonsful vegetable oil
6 fresh tomatoes or a 15 oz (425g) tin	6 fresh tomatoes or 1 medium-sized can
½ teaspoonful basil	½ teaspoonful basil
1 teaspoonful oregano	1 teaspoonful oregano
6 oz (150g) sweetcorn kernels	1 cupful sweetcorn kernels
2 potatoes, cooked and diced	2 potatoes, cooked and diced
4 medium green peppers	4 medium green peppers
2 oz (50g) grated Cheddar cheese	½ cupful grated Cheddar cheese

1. Plunge the macaroni into boiling water and cook until just soft, about 10 minutes.
2. Finely chop the onion and cook in the oil for 2 minutes over a low heat. Stir in the tomatoes (skinned if using fresh), the herbs and the sweetcorn. Cook for 10 minutes over a low heat.
3. Stir the cooked macaroni and potato into the sauce and cook for a further 5 minutes. The sauce should be thick and pulpy.
4. Cut the peppers in half lengthwise, remove the seeds and plunge the peppers into boiling water. Blanch for 2 minutes. Drain well and arrange on an ovenproof dish.
5. Divide the filling between the shells and sprinkle the grated cheese over the top. Pop under a hot grill for a couple of minutes until the cheese has melted and is bubbling. Serve at once.

SAVOURY CRUMBLE

Serves 4. Supplies 9.5g protein/305 calories per portion.

Imperial (Metric)	American
3 oz (75g) wholemeal flour	¾ cupful wholewheat flour
1 oz (25g) walnuts	¼ cupful English walnuts
2 tablespoonsful sesame seeds	2 tablespoonsful sesame seeds
2 oz (50g) soft vegetable margarine	5 tablespoonsful soft vegetable margarine
2 oz (50g) grated strong Cheddar	½ cupful grated strong Cheddar
1¼ lb (550g) mixed root vegetables all finely diced	1¼ pounds mixed root vegetables all finely diced
1 large onion, finely chopped	1 large onion, finely chopped
1 tablespoonful oil	1 tablespoonful oil
1 tablespoonful wholemeal flour	1 tablespoonful wholewheat flour
¼ pint (150ml) tomato juice	⅔ cupful tomato juice
¼ pint (150ml) water or vegetable stock	⅔ cupful water or vegetable stock
½ teaspoonful oregano	½ teaspoonful oregano
1 tablespoonful chopped parsley	1 tablespoonful chopped parsley
Sea salt	Sea salt
Freshly ground black pepper	Freshly ground black pepper

1. Rub the margarine into the flour, nuts and seeds. Stir in the cheese.
2. *Sauté* the prepared vegetables and onion in the oil for few minutes. Sprinkle in the flour and stir in well then gradually add the juice and water or stock. Stir well and bring to the boil. Reduce heat and simmer for 10 minutes.
3. Remove from heat, add herbs and season. Place in base of an ovenproof dish and cover with topping, smooth over evenly and then bake in a pre-heated oven at 400°F/200°C (Gas Mark 6) for 25 minutes.

NUTTY MARROW RINGS

Serves 4. Supplies 6.5g protein/190 calories per portion.

Imperial (Metric)
1 large marrow
3 oz (75g) walnuts
3 oz (75g) fresh wholemeal breadcrumbs
1 onion
Handful fresh parsley
2 oz (50g) mushrooms
1 egg, beaten
Sea salt
Freshly ground black pepper

American
1 large summer squash
⅔ cupful English walnuts
1½ cupsful fresh wholewheat breadcrumbs
1 onion
Handful fresh parsley
1 cupful mushrooms
1 egg, beaten
Sea salt
Freshly ground black pepper

1. Cut the marrow (squash) into 1 in. (2cm) thick slices. Using a teaspoon, carefully scoop out the seeds from the centre. Plunge into boiling water or steam until just tender (about 10 minutes) don't let it become mushy.
2. Meanwhile, finely grind the walnuts or chop very finely. Finely chop the onion, parsley and mushrooms. Mix these with the nuts and breadcrumbs, add the beaten egg and season lightly. Mix in well.
3. Arrange the marrow (squash) rings on an ovenproof dish and stuff the centres, pressing the mixture in firmly. Spoon a couple of tablespoonsful of cold water around the rings and cover with foil. Bake for 20 minutes at 350°F/180°C (Gas Mark 4).

NUTTY BURGERS

Serves 4. Supplies 7g protein/250 calories per portion.

Vary this basic recipe with different nuts of your choice or with oatmeal in place of the breadcrumbs. The protein is perfectly balanced to give a nutritious and tasty alternative to beefburgers.

Imperial (Metric)	**American**
1 oz (25g) sunflower seeds	¼ cupful sunflower seeds
2 oz (50g) walnuts	½ cupful English walnuts
4 oz (100g) fresh wholemeal breadcrumbs	2 cupsful fresh wholewheat breadcrumbs
1 large onion	1 large onion
2 oz (50g) mushrooms	1 cupful mushrooms
½ small green pepper	½ small green pepper
2 tablespoonsful oil	2 tablespoonsful oil
1 oz (25g) strong Cheddar cheese, finely grated	¼ cupful finely grated strong Cheddar cheese
1 tablespoonful soya sauce	1 tablespoonful soy sauce
1 tablespoonful lemon juice	1 tablespoonful lemon juice
Handful chopped parsley	Handful chopped parsley
Tahini to bind	Tahini to bind
Sea salt	Sea salt
Freshly ground black pepper	Freshly ground black pepper

1. Finely grind the seeds and nuts. Mix together with ¾ of the breadcrumbs. Set the remaining breadcrumbs aside.
2. Finely chop the onion, mushrooms and pepper. Cook together in a smear of the oil for few minutes until soft, but not brown.
3. Stir in the onion mixture with the seeds, nuts and breadcrumbs. Add the Cheddar, the soya sauce, lemon juice and parsley. Add a little tahini to bind if needed and season lightly.
4. Divide the mixture into four. Shape into burgers and dip in the remaining breadcrumbs. Heat the remaining oil in a frying pan and quickly cook each burger until golden brown on both sides.

CASHEW RICE

Serves 4. Supplies 10.5g protein/400 calories per portion.

Imperial (Metric)	American
1 large onion	1 large onion
1 large carrot	1 large carrot
1 clove garlic	1 clove garlic
1 tablespoonful vegetable oil	1 tablespoonful vegetable oil
½ lb (¼ kilo) long-grain brown rice	1 cupful long-grain brown rice
1 small cauliflower	1 small cauliflower
1 bay leaf	1 bay leaf
1 pint (½ litre) water	2½ cupsful water
2 courgettes	2 zucchini
4 oz (100g) cashew nuts	¾ cupful cashew nuts
Sea salt	Sea salt
Freshly ground black pepper	Freshly ground black pepper

1. Finely chop the onion, dice the carrot and crush the garlic. Cook together in the oil for 3 minutes. Stir in the rice and cook for a few minutes until the grains are transparent.

2. Stir in the cauliflower florets and then add the bay leaf and water. Bring to the boil then reduce heat, cover and simmer for 10 minutes. At this stage stir in the thinly sliced courgettes (zucchini) and continue to cook for a further 15 minutes, when the rice should be just tender and the liquid absorbed. Season to taste.

3. Just before serving lightly roast the cashew nuts — the quickest way is to heat in a heavy-based frying pan (skillet) for a couple of minutes with a smear of oil. The nuts should just turn golden. Stir into the rice. Serve hot or cold with a crisp green salad.

SUNBURST RISOTTO

Serves 4. Supplies 10g protein/190 calories per portion.

Imperial (Metric)	**American**
1 large onion	1 large onion
6 oz (150g) carrots	2 medium carrots
1 tablespoonful oil	1 tablespoonful oil
½ lb (¼ kilo) long-grain brown rice	1 cupful long-grain brown rice
¾ pint (400ml) water	2 cupsful water
1 green pepper	1 green pepper
4 oz (100g) mushrooms	2 cupsful mushrooms
4 oz (100g) sunflower seeds	1 cupful sunflower seeds
Sea salt	Sea salt
Freshly ground black pepper	Freshly ground black pepper

1. Finely chop the onion, finely dice the carrots and cook together in the oil for 3 minutes.
2. Stir in the rice and cook for 2 minutes until grains are transparent. Add the water, bring to the boil, then reduce heat, cover and cook for 25 minutes.
3. While rice is cooking, fiinely chop the pepper, slice the mushrooms and toast the sunflower seeds under a hot grill until just turning golden.
4. Stir these ingredients into the rice and test to see if the rice is cooked. The grains should just be soft. If not, continue cooking until ready. If there is excess fluid, turn up heat and drive off by heating fiercely for a few minutes. Season to taste and serve.

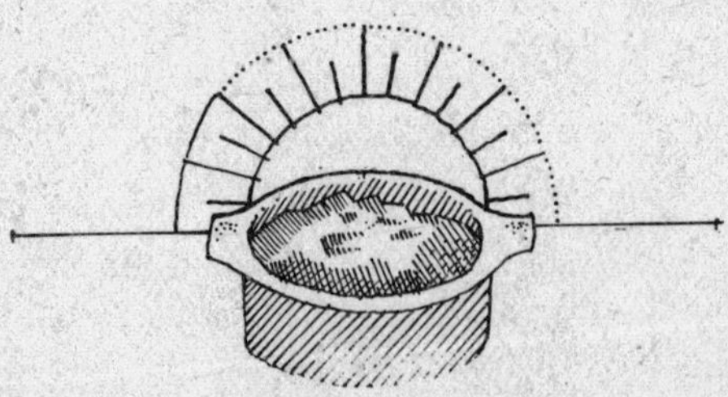

LENTIL PIE

Serves 4. Supplies 12g protein/305 calories per portion.

A vegetarian version of shepherd's pie made with a rich lentil sauce.

Imperial (Metric)	**American**
1 stick celery	1 stalk celery
1 large onion	1 large onion
2 cloves garlic	2 cloves garlic
2 carrots	2 carrots
1 tablespoonful oil	1 tablespoonful oil
1 red pepper	1 red pepper
1 lb (½ kilo) fresh tomatoes or 15 oz (425g) tin	1 pound fresh tomatoes or 1 medium can
½ teaspoonful basil	½ teaspoonful basil
5 oz (125g) red lentils	¾ cupful red lentils
½ pint (¼ litre) water	1⅓ cupsful water
Sea salt	Sea salt
Freshly ground black pepper	Freshly ground black pepper
1½ lb (¾ kilo) potatoes	1½ pounds potatoes
1 oz (25g) butter or soft vegetable margarine	2½ tablespoonsful butter or soft vegetable margarine

1. Finely chop the celery and onion and crush the garlic. Scrub and finely dice the carrots. *Sauté* all together in the oil for 3 minutes.
2. Finely chop the red pepper and add to pan with tomatoes (skinned if using fresh). Add the basil, lentils and water and stir in thoroughly. Bring to the boil, then reduce heat, cover and simmer until soft (about 30 minutes). You may need to add extra water as the lentils cook.
3. While the lentils are cooking, peel or scrub the potatoes, cut into chunks and cook until soft. Mash with the butter or margarine and add a little milk if necessary.
4. Season the lentil mixture and place in an ovenproof dish. Top with the potato, smooth over and pop under a hot grill to brown the topping.

KHICHHARI

Serves 4. Supplies 13.5g protein/380 calories per portion.

A traditional blend of lentils, rice and spices said to have been the inspiration for our own kedgeree. A meal in itself.

Imperial (Metric)

¾ lb (350g) carrots
2 large onions
1 clove garlic
1 tablespoonful oil
1 teaspoonful cumin seeds
1½ teaspoonsful ground coriander
1 teaspoonful garam masala
1 teaspoonful turmeric
Pinch paprika
Pinch nutmeg
½ lb (¼ kilo) long-grain brown rice
1¾ pints (900ml) vegetable stock or water
5 oz (125g) red lentils
Sea salt
Freshly ground black pepper

American

12 ounces carrots
2 large onions
1 clove garlic
1 tablespoonful oil
1 teaspoonful cumin seeds
1½ teaspoonsful ground coriander
1 teaspoonful garam masala
1 teaspoonful turmeric
Pinch paprika
Pinch nutmeg
1 cupful long-grain brown rice
4½ cupsful vegetable stock or water
¾ cupful red lentils
Sea salt
Freshly ground black pepper

1. Scrub and finely dice the carrots, finely chop the onion and crush the garlic. Cook together in the oil for 2 minutes.
2. Stir in the spices and cook a further minute. Then add the rice and stir in well, cooking until the grains turn transparent (about a minute).
3. Stir in the stock or water and the lentils and a little seasoning. Bring to the boil, cover tightly and reduce heat. Cook for around 30 minutes until the rice is just tender and all the fluid absorbed.

HARICOT BEAN GOULASH

Serves 5. Supplies 13g protein/260 calories per portion.

Imperial (Metric)	**American**
6 oz (150g) haricot beans, soaked overnight	¾ cupful navy beans, soaked overnight
4 oz (100g) wholemeal macaroni	1 cupful wholewheat macaroni
3 large onions	3 large onions
4 cloves garlic	4 cloves garlic
1 large green pepper	1 large green pepper
4 oz (100g) mushrooms	2 cupsful mushrooms
3 courgettes	3 zucchini
6 oz (150g) sweetcorn kernels	1 cupful sweetcorn kernels
1 tablespoonful oil	1 tablespoonful oil
15 oz (425g) tin or 1 lb (½ kilo) fresh tomatoes	1 medium can or 1 pound fresh tomatoes
4 tablespoonsful tomato *purée*	⅓ cupful tomato paste
1 tablespoonful paprika	1 tablespoonful paprika
1 teaspoonful oregano	1 teaspoonful oregano
Sea salt	Sea salt
Freshly ground black pepper	Freshly ground black pepper

1. Drain the beans and cook in fresh water until soft (about 1 hour). Cook the macaroni in boiling water for about 10 minutes until just soft. (These can both be cooked in advance to save time.)

2. Finely chop the onions and crush the garlic. Finely chop the pepper. Slice the mushrooms and courgettes (zucchini). If using fresh tomatoes, skin and chop.

3. Cook the onion and garlic in the oil for 2 minutes. Then stir in the peppers, mushrooms, courgettes (zucchini), sweetcorn. Add the tomatoes and the tomato *purée*, paprika and oregano. Bring to the boil, then add the cooked and drained beans and pasta, reduce heat and simmer for 15 minutes. Season to taste and serve.

CURRIED POTATOES

Serves 8. Supplies 4.5g protein/130 calories per portion.

Hot and spicy. Serve these with a mild vegetable curry and rice or an Indian bread. The yogurt completes the protein. Leave out the chilli powder if you don't like your curry too hot.

Imperial (Metric)	American
2 lb (1 kilo) potatoes	6 medium potatoes
1 onion	1 onion
2 cloves garlic	2 cloves garlic
1 tablespoonful oil	1 tablespoonful oil
1 teaspoonful ground coriander	1 teaspoonful ground coriander
1 teaspoonful turmeric	1 teaspoonful turmeric
1 teaspoonful cumin seeds	1 teaspoonful cumin seeds
½ teaspoonful chilli powder (optional)	½ teaspoonful chilli powder (optional)
½ pint (300ml) yogurt	1⅓ cupsful yogurt
1 tablespoonful tomato *purée*	1 tablespoonful tomato paste
Chopped parsley or coriander to garnish	Chopped parsley or cilantro to garnish

1. Scrub the potatoes and cut into chunks. Place in boiling water and cook for 4 minutes. Cool and pierce with a trussing needle in a couple of places to let marinade seep in.
2. Finely chop the onion and crush the garlic. Cook together in the oil for 2 minutes. Add the coriander (cilantro), turmeric, cumin seeds, chilli powder (if using) and cook for a further 2 minutes. Remove from heat and stir in yogurt and tomato *purée*.
3. Place potatoes in a shallow ovenproof dish, pour over spicy mixture and leave to marinade for 2 hours, turning twice. Cover and bake in a pre-heated oven at 400°F/200°C (Gas Mark 6) for 30 minutes, basting a couple of times. Garnish and serve.

CAULIFLOWER CURRY

Serves 2. Supplies 7g protein/200 calories per portion.

Imperial (Metric)	**American**
2 onions	2 onions
1 clove garlic	1 clove garlic
2 tablespoonsful vegetable oil	2 tablespoonsful vegetable oil
½ teaspoonful turmeric	½ teaspoonful turmeric
½ teaspoonful chilli powder	½ teaspoonful chilli powder
2 tomatoes	2 tomatoes
1 teaspoonful ground coriander	1 teaspoonful ground coriander
1 teaspoonful ground cumin	1 teaspoonful ground cumin
1 large cauliflower	1 large cauliflower
2 tablespoonsful cold water	2 tablespoonsful cold water
1 teaspoonful garam masala	1 teaspoonful garam masala

1. Finely slice the onions and crush the garlic. *Sauté* together in the oil with the turmeric and chilli powder for 5 minutes.
2. Skin and chop the tomatoes and add to the pan with the coriander and cumin, stirring in thoroughly.
3. Divide cauliflower into florets, wash and then add to pan with the water, stir well and cover and cook for 20 minutes, stirring occasionally to prevent sticking. Add more water if needed.
4. Stir in the garam masala, turn off the heat and leave pan covered for 5 minutes to let flavours mingle.

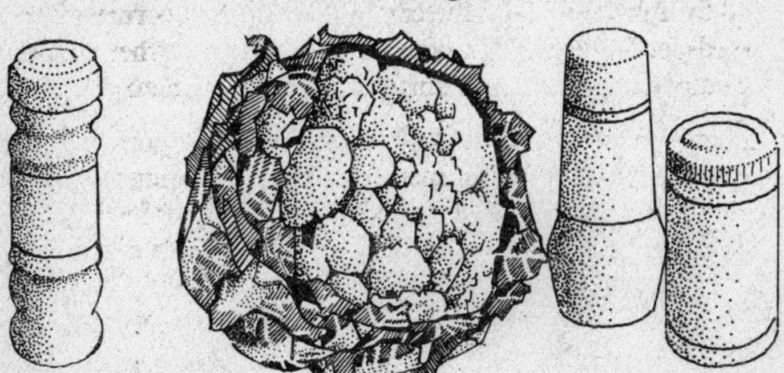

SPINACH AND PEPPER CURRY

Serves 4 and supplies 9g protein/160 calories per portion OR serves 6 and supplies 6g protein/107 calories.

Spinach is rich in minerals and vitamins and makes a tasty, smooth *purée*. Serve with other vegetable curries, or with a vegetable pulao.

Imperial (Metric)	American
1½ lb (¾ kilo) fresh spinach	1½ pounds fresh spinach
1 medium green pepper	1 medium green pepper
1½ tablespoonsful oil	1½ tablespoonsful oil
1 large onion	1 large onion
2 cloves garlic	2 cloves garlic
2 teaspoonsful ground cumin	2 teaspoonsful ground cumin
2 teaspoonsful ground coriander	2 teaspoonsful ground coriander
2 tablespoonsful tomato *purée*	2 tablespoonsful tomato paste
Freshly ground black pepper	Freshly ground black pepper

1. Break the stems from the spinach, wash thoroughly and then place the leaves in a pan with no extra water. Simmer over a low heat for 15 minutes. Drain, squeezing out surplus moisture, and then chop finely.
2. Core and de-seed the pepper and chop finely, and finely chop the onion. Crush the garlic.
3. Heat the oil and cook the onion and garlic and pepper until soft but without browning (about 5 minutes). Then add the spices and stir in thoroughly.
4. Add the chopped spinach and the tomato *purée* and cook over a high heat for 3 minutes to heat through. Season with black pepper and serve.

CHAPATIS

Makes 12. Each supplies 3g protein/70 calories.

Chapatis are simple to make and can help to balance the protein of vegetable curries. A good combination would be chapatis, Cauliflower Curry (page 81) and a Raita (page 86).

Imperial (Metric)	**American**
¾ lb (350g) wholemeal flour	3 cupsful wholewheat flour
1 teaspoonful sea salt	1 teaspoonful sea salt
About ½ pint (¼ litre) water	About 1⅓ cupsful water

1. Sieve 10 oz (300g)/1½ cupsful flour into a bowl with the salt. Mix to a loose dough by gradually adding the water. Pound and knead for several minutes as this helps to make a light bread. Cover and leave to stand for at least an hour.
2. Knead dough — you may need to add a little more water. Then divide the dough into 12 pieces. Roll each into a ball and, using some of the spare flour, flatten each.
3. If you have a griddle this is perfect for cooking chapatis, otherwise a heavy quality frying pan (skillet) will do. Heat the griddle or pan and place a chapati on it. Cook one side lightly, then turn over. Turn back again and help the chapati to balloon out by holding the sides with two wooden spoons — this helps to trap the air and forces the dough to rise up.
4. Place under a hot grill to dry out and keep warm while cooking the rest. (If using an ordinary pan do take care not to overheat it. Turn the heat down quite low after it has warmed through initially.)

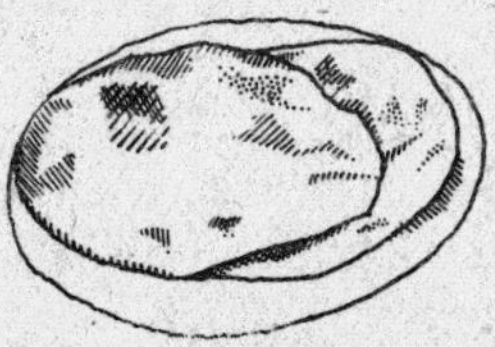

VEGETABLE BIRIANI

Serves 4. Supplies about 9g protein/280 calories if made with all these vegetables.

A complete vegetarian Indian meal in itself — or cut down on the vegetables and serve with some of the other vegetable curry dishes. To enhance the protein value of the dish add one of the suggested extras.

Imperial (Metric)	American
1½ tablespoonsful oil	1½ tablespoonsful oil
1 large onion, finely chopped	1 large onion, finely chopped
2 cloves garlic, crushed	2 cloves garlic, crushed
1 teaspoonful turmeric	1 teaspoonful turmeric
1 teaspoonful garam masala	1 teaspoonful garam masala
½ lb (¼ kilo) long-grain brown rice	1 cupful long-grain brown rice
1 pint (½ litre) water or vegetable stock	2½ cupsful water or vegetable stock

Vegetables to choose from:

Imperial (Metric)	American
2 carrots, diced	2 carrots, diced
1 medium potato, diced	1 medium potato, diced
1 small cauliflower, divided into florets	1 small cauliflower, divided into florets
3 courgettes, sliced	3 zucchini, sliced
1 small aubergine, diced and salted for 30 minutes	1 small eggplant, diced and salted for 30 minutes
1 medium green pepper	1 medium green pepper
4 oz (100g) fresh peas	⅔ cupful fresh peas
2 tomatoes, skinned and chopped	2 tomatoes, skinned and chopped
4 oz (100g) mushrooms, sliced	2 cupsful mushrooms, sliced

1. Heat the oil in a large pan. Cook the onion and garlic in the oil for 2 minutes. Add spices and cook a further minute. Stir in the rice and cook until the grains turn transparent. Add the stock or water and bring to the boil.

2. At this point add the following vegetables (if used): the carrot, potato, cauliflower, aubergine (eggplant), mushrooms, tomatoes.
3. Cover, reduce heat to a steady simmer and cook for 15 minutes.
4. Now add the peas and courgettes (zucchini) if used, continue to simmer until the rice is just soft, adding more liquid if required.
5. Just before serving stir in the chopped green pepper (if used).

Protein extras:
2 hard-boiled eggs (another 3g protein per portion)
2 oz (50g)/⅓ cupful cashew nuts or blanched almonds (another 2g protein per portion).

VEGETABLE SALAD

Serves 4. Supplies less than a gram of protein and around 14 calories.

A light accompaniment for any curried dish.

Imperial (Metric)	American
½ cucumber	½ cucumber
1 green pepper	1 green pepper
1 red pepper	1 red pepper
½ bunch spring onions	½ bunch scallions
1 teaspoonful olive oil	1 teaspoonful olive oil
1 tablespoonful lemon juice	1 tablespoonful lemon juice
Sea salt	Sea salt
Freshly ground black pepper	Freshly ground black pepper

1. Thinly slice the cucumber. Cut the peppers into fine strips about 2 in. (5cm) long. Chop the onions.
2. Arrange the vegetables in a dish. Shake together the oil, lemon juice and seasoning in a screw-top jar and pour over the vegetables.

BANANA RAITA

Serves 6. Supplies 1.8g protein/50 calories.

Raita is simply a name for a yogurt-based side dish. Use grated cucumbers, finely-chopped onions mixed with mint or *puréed* aubergines (eggplants). The yogurt also helps to balance the protein in vegetable curries.

Imperial (Metric)	American
2 large ripe bananas	2 large ripe bananas
¼ pint (150ml) yogurt	⅔ cupful yogurt

Cut the bananas into fine slices. Arrange around a dish and pour over the yogurt. Serve at once.

7.
VEGETABLES & SALADS

AVOCADO DIP

Serves 4. Supplies 2.8g protein/128 calories, per portion.

A light starter — serve with sticks of celery, peppers and carrots.

Imperial (Metric)	American
2 avocado pears	2 avocado pears
3 oz (75g) curd cheese	⅓ cupful curd cheese
2 tablespoonsful lemon juice	2 tablespoonsful lemon juice
1 tablespoonful finely chopped onion	1 tablespoonful finely chopped onion

1. Cut the avocadoes in half and remove the stones. Scoop out the flesh and mash with the remaining ingredients until fairly smooth.
2. Pile into a bowl and serve chilled.

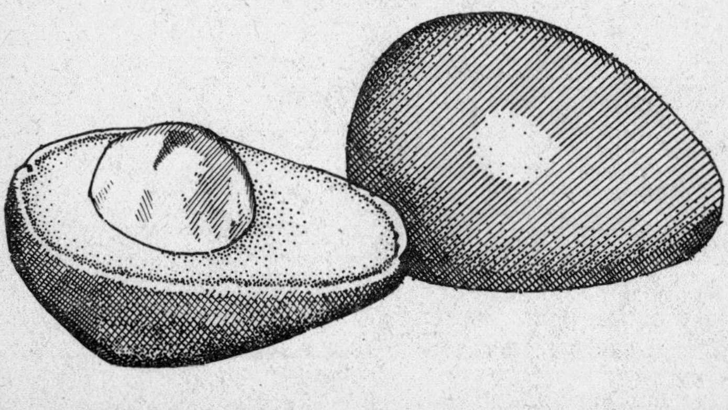

BEAN SALAD

Serves 6. Supplies 5g of protein/120 calories per portion.

Mix together beans of different shapes and colours. The pasta balances the protein.

Imperial (Metric)	American
3 oz (75g) red kidney beans, soaked overnight	½ cupful red kidney beans, soaked overnight
3 oz (75g) flageolets, soaked overnight	½ cupful flageolets, soaked overnight
2 oz (50g) wholemeal pasta rings	½ cupful wholewheat pasta rings
1 leek	1 leek
2 tablespoonsful oil	2 tablespoonsful oil
1 tablespoonful cider vinegar	1 tablespoonful cider vinegar
Pinch paprika	Pinch paprika
Sea salt	Sea salt
Freshly ground black pepper	Freshly ground black pepper

1. Cook the beans until just soft.
2. Cook the pasta until just soft. Finely slice the leek.
3. In a screw-top jar shake together the oil, vinegar, paprika and seasoning.
4. Mix the beans, pasta and leeks and pour over dressing. If you dress the beans and pasta while still hot, the dressing will soak in better and give more flavour.

BROAD BEANS IN YOGURT

Serves 6. Supplies 6g protein/99 calories per portion.

Imperial (Metric)	American
2 lb (1 kilo) broad beans	2 pounds Windsor beans
3 fl oz (85ml) natural yogurt	⅓ cupful natural yogurt
1 tablespoonful oil	1 tablespoonful oil
Juice of a lemon	Juice of a lemon
2 tablespoonsful chopped parsley	2 tablespoonsful chopped parsley
Sea salt	Sea salt
Freshly ground black pepper	Freshly ground black pepper

1. Shell the beans and cook in a little boiling water, or steam until just tender.
2. Drain and pour over the yogurt. Mix together the oil and lemon juice, season and add to the bean mixture with the parsley. Mix in well and chill.

COLESLAW

Serves 6. Supplies 2.4g protein/120 calories per portion.

There is no comparison between bought and home-made!

Imperial (Metric)	**American**
1 small white cabbage	1 small white cabbage
2 carrots	2 carrots
2 red-skinned eating apples	2 red-skinned eating apples
1 tablespoonful lemon juice	1 tablespoonful lemon juice
1 small onion	1 small onion
½ green pepper	½ green pepper
4 oz (100g) raisins	⅔ cupful raisins
1 tablespoonful finely-chopped parsley	1 tablespoonful finely-chopped parsley
2 tablespoonsful mayonnaise	2 tablespoonsful mayonnaise
2 tablespoonsful natural yogurt	2 tablespoonsful natural yogurt
Sea salt	Sea salt
Freshly ground black pepper	Freshly ground black pepper

1. Grate or finely shred the cabbage. Grate the carrots.
2. Finely dice the apples, leaving the peel on. Cover with the lemon juice. Finely chop the onion and pepper. Mix all the vegetables, apples, parsley and raisins together.
3. Pour over the mayonnaise and yogurt — adding a little more of each if required. The vegetables should just be lightly coated in the dressing. Season to taste, chill.

RED AND GREEN SALAD

Serves 6. Supplies roughly 3g protein and 100 calories per portion.

Imperial (Metric)	American
½ small white cabbage	½ small white cabbage
1 small cooked beetroot	1 small cooked beetroot
3 small young carrots	3 small young carrots
6 oz (150g) runner beans	6 ounces green beans
1 red pepper	1 red pepper
1 green pepper	1 green pepper
1 bunch watercress	1 bunch watercress
½ bunch spring onions	½ bunch scallions
3 tablespoonsful oil	3 tablespoonsful oil
1 tablespoonful white wine vinegar	1 tablespoonful white wine vinegar
Crushed clove garlic	Crushed clove garlic
Sea salt	Sea salt
Freshly ground black pepper	Freshly ground black pepper
2 tomatoes, finely chopped	2 tomatoes, finely chopped
1 tablespoonful finely chopped parsley	1 tablespoonful finely chopped parsley

1. Finely shred the cabbage. Cut the beetroot into fine matchsticks and grate the carrots. Cut the beans into 2 in. (5cm) lengths and cook until just soft.
2. Core the peppers and cut into fine strips. Wash the watercress and discard any yellow leaves. Finely chop the onions.
3. Mix together the carrot and cabbage and arrange in a salad bowl. Arrange remaining vegetables on top. Shake together the oil, vinegar, garlic and seasoning and pour over salad. Arrange tomatoes and parsley on top.

CABBAGE SAUTÉ

Serves 6. Supplies 1g protein/87 calories per portion.

Imperial (Metric)
1 medium white cabbage
2 oz (50g) butter or soft vegetable margarine
1 large onion, finely chopped
1 clove
Sea salt
Freshly ground black pepper

American
1 medium white cabbage
¼ cupful butter or soft vegetable margarine
1 large onion, finely chopped
1 clove
Sea salt
Freshly ground black pepper

1. Cut cabbage in four, wash thoroughly and cut away the core. Finely shred.
2. Plunge into a little boiling water and cook for 3 minutes. Drain well, reserving liquid for stock. Melt butter or margarine in a pan and *sauté* the finely chopped onion for 2 minutes. Stir in the cabbage, add the clove, cover and cook for 5 minutes. Remove the clove and season with plenty of freshly ground black pepper.

CREAMY CARROT SALAD

Serves 5. Supplies 1.9g protein/39 calories per portion.

Imperial (Metric)	American
1 lb (½ kilo) carrots	1 pound carrots
4 fl oz (120ml) natural yogurt	⅔ cupful natural yogurt
1 tablespoonful single cream	1 tablespoonful light cream
Sea salt	Sea salt
Freshly ground black pepper	Freshly ground black pepper
1 tablespoonful finely chopped parsley	1 tablespoonful finely chopped parsley

1. Scrub and finely grate the carrots.
2. Mix the yogurt with the cream and then pour over the carrots. Toss together well and then season lightly. Sprinkle parsley on top as garnish. Chill.

CAULIFLOWER PASTA SALAD

Serves 6. Supplies 6g protein/160 calories per portion.

Imperial (Metric)	American
6 oz (150g) wholemeal pasta spirals or rings	1½ cupsful wholewheat pasta spirals or rings
1 large cauliflower	1 large cauliflower
1 green pepper	1 green pepper
2 courgettes	2 zucchini
¼ cucumber	¼ cucumber

Dressing:

Imperial (Metric)	American
2 tablespoonsful oil	2 tablespoonsful oil
1 tablespoonful white wine vinegar	1 tablespoonful white wine vinegar
1 tablespoonful chopped chives	1 tablespoonful chopped chives
Sea salt	Sea salt
Freshly ground black pepper	Freshly ground black pepper

1. Cook the pasta in boiling water for 10-12 minutes until just soft.
2. Meanwhile prepare the vegetables. Divide the cauliflower into florets. Finely chop the pepper. Cut the courgettes (zucchini) into ½ in. (1cm) thick slices, and then cut each into quarters. Steam or lightly boil for 2 minutes. Finely dice the cucumber.
3. Mix all ingredients together. Prepare the dressing. In a screw top jar shake together the oil, vinegar, chives and seasoning. Pour over salad and serve.

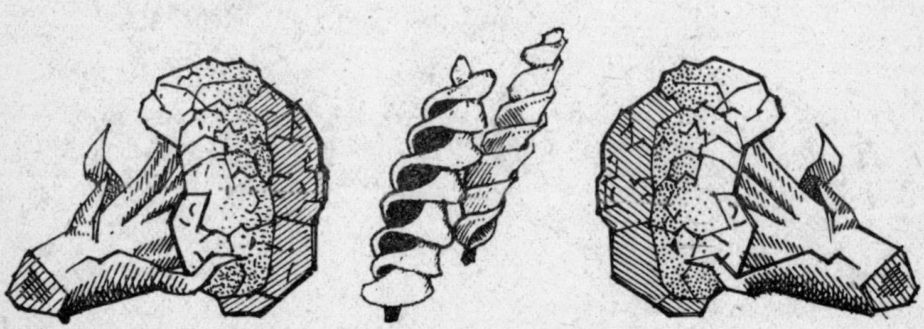

BRAISED CELERY

Serves 5. Supplies 1.2g protein/58 calories per portion.

Imperial (Metric)
1 head celery
2 carrots
1 large onion
1 oz (25g) butter or soft vegetable margarine
½ pint (¼ litre) water or vegetable stock
1 teaspoonful lemon juice

American
1 head celery
2 carrots
1 large onion
2½ tablespoonsful butter or soft vegetable margarine
1⅓ cupsful water or vegetable stock
1 teaspoonful lemon juice

1. Pull apart the celery and cut into 1 in. (2cm) pieces. Scrub and thinly slice the carrots. Peel and finely chop the onion.
2. Blanch the celery in boiling water for 2 minutes. Drain and arrange with carrots and onion in a casserole dish. Dot with butter or margarine and pour over stock or water and lemon juice.
3. Cover with foil and bake at 400°F/200°C (Gas Mark 6) for 40 minutes.

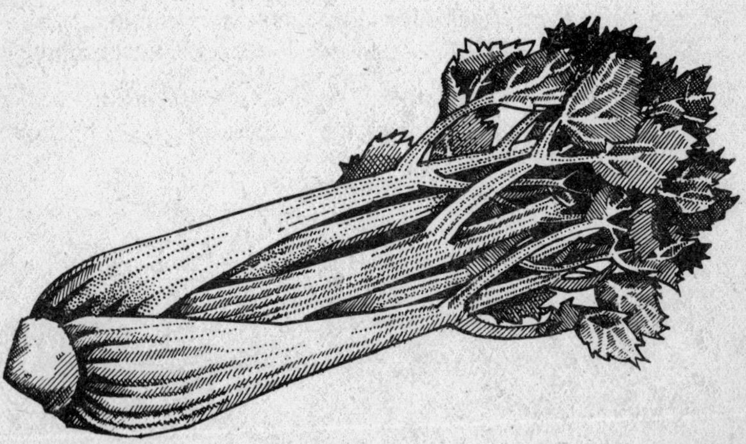

CRACKED WHEAT SALAD

Serves 6. Supplies 2.3g protein/90 calories per portion.

An unusual combination of mint, parsley and lemon juice give this salad a distinctive flavour — very refreshing.

Imperial (Metric)
4 oz (100g) cracked wheat
2 tablespoonsful chopped spring onions
4 tablespoonsful finely chopped parsley
3 tablespoonsful finely chopped mint
2 tomatoes, finely chopped
2 tablespoonsful olive oil
2 tablespoonsful lemon juice
Sea salt
Freshly ground black pepper
A few black olives

American
2/3 cupful cracked wheat
2 tablespoonsful finely chopped scallions
1/3 cupful finely chopped parsley
3 tablespoonsful finely chopped mint
2 tomatoes, finely chopped
2 tablespoonsful olive oil
2 tablespoonsful lemon juice
Sea salt
Freshly ground black pepper
A few black olives

1. Place the cracked wheat in a bowl and cover with cold water. Leave to stand for 30 minutes. Then drain and wrap in a tea towel and squeeze out excess moisture. Tip into a salad bowl.
2. Stir in next four ingredients. Shake together the oil and lemon juice in a screw-top jar. Pour over salad and toss thoroughly. Season to taste and garnish with a few black olives.

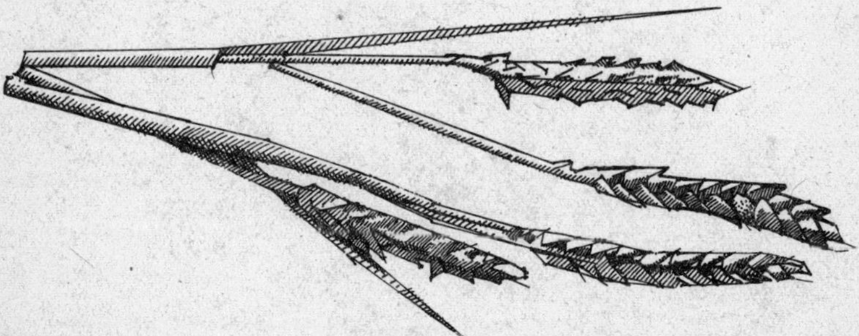

GREEN SALAD

Serves 6. Supplies under a gram of protein and about 50 calories per portion.

Imperial (Metric)
1 crisp lettuce
1 clove garlic
2 tablespoonsful olive oil
1 dessertspoonful white wine vinegar
1 tablespoonful chopped chives
Sea salt
Freshly ground black pepper

American
1 crisp lettuce
1 clove garlic
2 tablespoonsful olive oil
2 teaspoonsful white wine vinegar
1 tablespoonful chopped chives
Sea salt
Freshly ground black pepper

1. Remove any damaged outer leaves from the lettuce. Carefully wash under a running tap. Shake well.
2. Rub the garlic clove around a wooden salad bowl. In a screw top jar shake together the remaining ingredients to form a dressing.
3. Arrange lettuce in bowl and pour over dressing — toss thoroughly and serve at once.

MUSHROOM SALAD

Serves 4. Supplies just under 1g protein/50 calories per portion.

Imperial (Metric)	**American**
4 oz (100g) button mushrooms	2 cupsful button mushrooms
1 bunch watercress	1 bunch watercress
1 clove garlic	1 clove garlic
Juice of a lemon	Juice of a lemon
2 tablespoonsful olive oil	2 tablespoonsful olive oil
1 dessertspoonful cider vinegar	2 teaspoonsful cider vinegar
Freshly ground black pepper	Freshly ground black pepper

1. Wipe the mushrooms and cut into neat even slices. Wash the watercress and remove any thick or yellowing stalks. Arrange in a salad bowl.

2. Crush garlic and place in a screw-top jar with the oil and vinegar and pepper and shake together. Pour over mushrooms ensuring all are evenly coated. Then transfer mushrooms to the bed of watercress and serve.

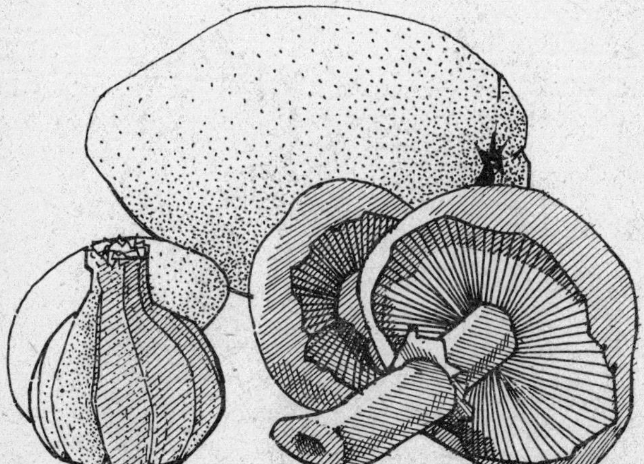

PASTA SALAD

Serves 5. Supplies 2.5g protein/150 calories per portion.

Imperial (Metric)	American
4 oz (100g) wholemeal pasta rings	1 cupful wholewheat pasta rings
1 green pepper	1 green pepper
A few black olives	A few black olives
3 tomatoes	3 tomatoes
1 clove garlic	1 clove garlic
3 tablespoonsful olive oil	3 tablespoonsful olive oil
1 tablespoonful white wine vinegar	1 tablespoonful white wine vinegar
Sea salt	Sea Salt
Freshly ground black pepper	Freshly ground black pepper

1. Cook the pasta until just soft (about 10-12 minutes). Drain.
2. Cut the pepper into fine strips about 1 in. (2cm) long. Cut the tomatoes into very thin segments and halve the olives. Mix in with the pasta.
3. Crush the garlic clove and place in a screw top jar with the oil, vinegar and seasoning. Shake together vigorously and pour over pasta and vegetables. Toss together and serve.

NEW POTATOES

Serves 6. Supplies 2.4g protein/150 calories per portion.

Potatoes are at their best when freshly dug and new — vitamin C is at its peak.

Imperial (Metric)	**American**
2 lb (1 kilo) new potatoes	2 pounds new potatoes
A few sprigs mint	A few sprigs mint
1 oz (25g) butter or soft vegetable margarine	2½ tablespoonsful butter or soft vegetable margarine
Sea salt	Sea salt
Freshly ground black pepper	Freshly ground black pepper

1. Gently rub dirt from the potatoes without damaging the skins.
2. Place in cold water with half the mint. Bring to the boil and cook for 20-25 minutes, until just tender. Drain and place in serving dish — dab butter on top and garnish with remaining mint, finely chopped.

LAYERED POTATOES

Serves 4-5. Supplies around 3g protein/160 calories per portion.

Imperial (Metric)	American
1½ lb (¾ kilo) potatoes	1½ pounds potatoes
1 onion	1 onion
1 small green pepper	1 small green pepper
½ pint (¼ litre) stock	1¼ cupsful stock
Sea salt	Sea salt
Freshly ground black pepper	Freshly ground black pepper
Knob of butter	Knob of butter

1. Scrub the potatoes and thinly slice into rounds. Finely chop the onion and pepper.

2. Rub the butter around the sides and base of a shallow ovenproof dish. Layer the potatoes, onions and pepper, finishing with a layer of potatoes. Pour over stock, season and cover with foil. Bake at 350°F/180°C (Gas Mark 4) for 50 minutes.

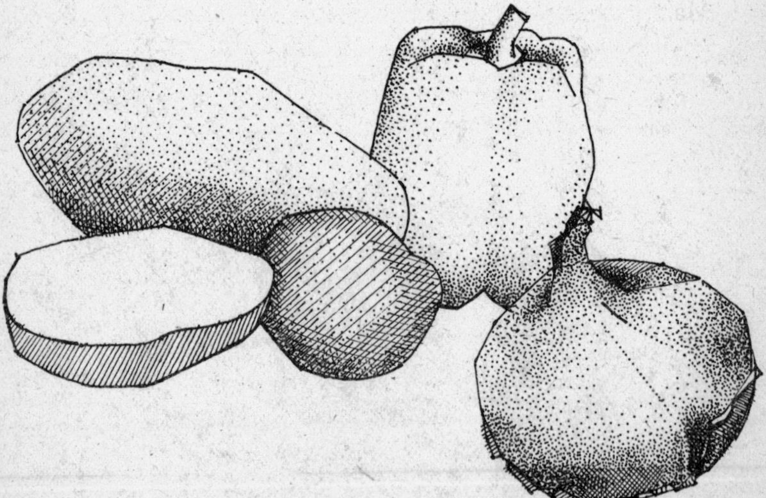

POTATOES ANNA

Serves 4. Supplies around 2g protein/130 calories per portion.

A simpler version, in which the potatoes are cooked alone with butter or soft vegetable margarine. For special occasions, the flavour of butter is hard to beat.

Imperial (Metric)	American
1 lb (½ kilo) potatoes	1 pound potatoes
1½ oz (40g) butter or soft vegetable margarine	3½ tablespoonsful butter or soft vegetable margarine
Sea salt	Sea salt
Freshly ground black pepper	Freshly ground black pepper

1. Scrub the potatoes, cut into fine rounds and pat dry.
2. Rub some of the fat around a small ovenproof dish.
3. Arrange the potatoes in neat overlapping circles, seasoning well and adding the remaining butter gradually.
4. Cover with foil and bake for 50 minutes at 350°F/180°C (Gas Mark 4). Sprinkle finely chopped parsley on top.

POTATO PURÉE

Serves 6. Supplies 3g protein/140 calories per portion.

Transform simple mashed potatoes into something special — pipe the *purée* and then bake.

Imperial (Metric)
1½ lb (¾ kilo) potatoes
1 onion
2 bay leaves
1 oz (25g) butter or soft vegetable margarine
2½ fl oz (75ml) milk, warmed
A little beaten egg

American
1½ pounds potatoes
1 onion
2 bay leaves
2½ tablespoonsful butter or soft vegetable margarine
⅓ cupful milk, warmed
A little beaten egg

1. Peel the potatoes. Cut into small chunks and place in a saucepan of cold water, add the onion and bay leaves. Bring to the boil, reduce heat slightly and cook until potatoes are just soft (about 20 minutes).
2. Strain immediately, discard the onion and bay leaves and rub potatoes through a fine sieve. Mix in the butter and warmed milk.
3. Fill a piping bag and, using a star nozzle, pipe spirals onto a lightly greased baking tray. Gently brush with egg yolk and bake in a pre-heated oven 400°F/200°C (Gas Mark 6) for 10 minutes. Glaze again with egg and return to oven for another 10 minutes — the spirals should turn a rich golden colour.

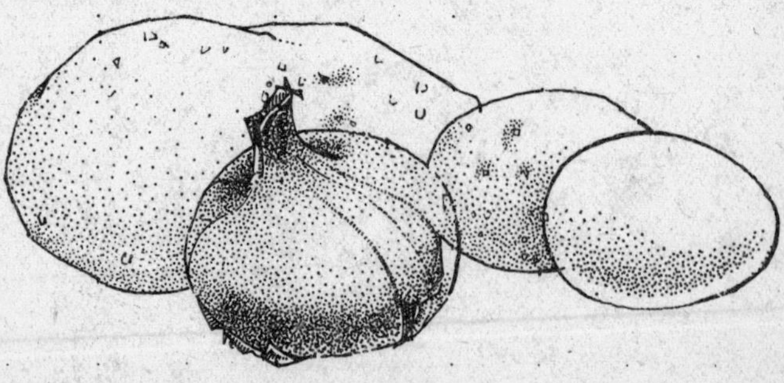

BAKED POTATOES

Baked potatoes are simple to prepare and topped with a little butter are the perfect accompaniment to many meals. Choose larger potatoes, add a filling, serve with a green salad and a bread roll and you have a sustaining meal. Here are a few ideas for tasty fillings which don't depend on protein-rich cheese for flavour. Prepare your potatoes by allowing a blemish-free, well-scrubbed potato weighing ½ lb (¼ kilo) per person. Bake in a pre-heated oven 400°F/200°C (Gas Mark 6) for 1 hour. Then add your filling.

Mushroom Magic

Enough for one filled potato. Supplies 5.5g protein/300 calories.

Imperial (Metric)	American
1 baked potato	1 baked potato
2 oz (50g) mushrooms	1 cupful mushrooms
1 clove garlic	1 clove garlic
Smear oil	Smear oil
1 dessertspoonful chopped parsley	2 teaspoonsful chopped parsley
Freshly ground black pepper	Freshly ground black pepper

1. When potato is nearly cooked, finely chop the mushrooms and crush the garlic. Cook together gently in the oil for a few minutes.
2. When potato is ready, cut in half. Carefully scoop out the flesh and mash. Blend in the mushroom mixture, parsley and pepper. Pile back into the potato skins and place in the oven for 10 minutes to reheat.

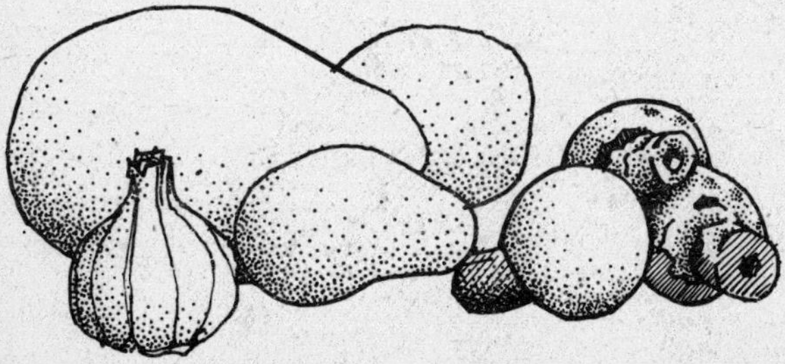

Peperoni Potato

Enough for one filled potato. Supplies 5.5g protein/290 calories.

Imperial (Metric)	American
1 baked potato	1 baked potato
½ green pepper	½ green pepper
1 small onion	1 small onion
Smear oil	Smear oil
1 tablespoonful tomato *purée*	1 tablespoonful tomato paste
½ teaspoonful oregano	½ teaspoonful oregano

1. When potato is nearly cooked, prepare the topping. Finely slice the onions and pepper and cook together for 2 minutes. Stir in the tomato *purée* and oregano and season.
2. Cut a deep cross on the potato and pile pepper mixture in. Serve at once.

Creamy Herb Potato

Supplies 5.5g protein/250 calories.

Choose a mixture of preferably fresh herbs — chives, parsley, garlic, mint, sage, a little chopped onion. Mix with a tablespoon of single (light) cream and freshly ground black pepper and when potato is cooked, scoop out flesh and blend in the herbs. Return to shells and serve at once.

Golden Delight

Supplies 7.5g protein/290 calories.

Finely chop half a hard-boiled egg and mix with some finely chopped chives. When potato is cooked, scoop out flesh and mix with the egg and chives and a knob of butter, add some freshly ground black pepper and return to shells. Serve at once.

POTATO SALAD

Serves 6. Supplies 2.7g protein/170 calories per portion.

Imperial (Metric)	**American**
1½ lb (¾ kilo) waxy potatoes	1½ pounds waxy potatoes
4 tablespoonsful mayonnaise	⅓ cupful mayonnaise
1 crushed garlic clove	1 crushed garlic clove
½ bunch spring onions	½ bunch scallions
1 tablespoonful chopped mint	1 tablespoonful chopped mint

1. Cook the potatoes until tender. Dice evenly and while still hot toss in the mayonnaise.
2. Finely chop the spring onions (scallions) and stir with the garlic into the mixture. Serve topped with chopped mint.

SPICY POTATO SALAD

Serves 8. Supplies 2.4g/136 calories per portion.

Imperial (Metric)	American
1½ lb (¾ kilo) small new potatoes	1½ pounds small new potatoes
1 clove garlic	1 clove garlic
1 teaspoonful cumin	1 teaspoonful cumin
1 teaspoonful ground coriander	1 teaspoonful ground coriander
1 tablespoonful poppy seeds	1 tablespoonful poppy seeds
3 tablespoonsful olive oil	3 tablespoonsful olive oil
1½ tablespoonsful cider vinegar	1½ tablespoonsful cider vinegar

1. Lightly rub dirt from the potatoes. Boil in their skins for 20 minutes or until tender.

2. Prepare the dressing, crush the garlic, beat with the cumin, coriander, poppy seeds, oil and vinegar. Shake well together and pour over the hot, cooked potatoes. Chill, toss again and serve.

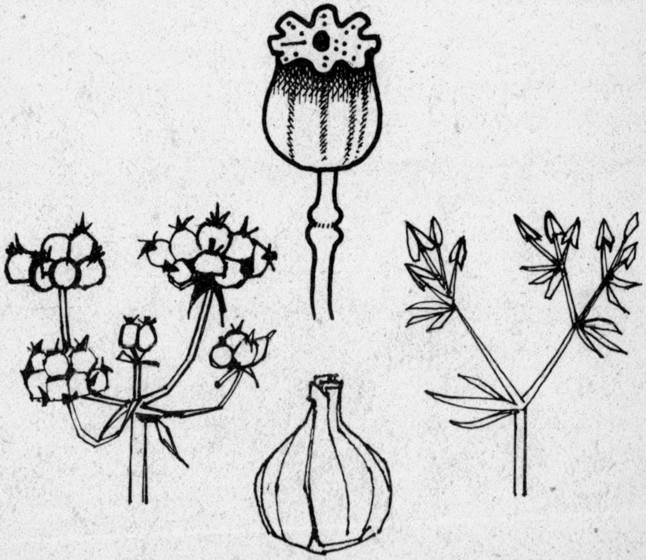

RATATOUILLE

4 generous servings. Supplies 3.5g protein/140 calories per portion.

Make this in the summer when these Mediterranean vegetables are in plentiful supply. A perfect starter served chilled, or serve as a side dish or as a main course with a savoury rice.

Imperial (Metric)	American
2 large aubergines	2 large eggplants
2 large onions	2 large onions
4 cloves garlic	4 cloves garlic
2 tablespoonsful olive oil	2 tablespoonsful olive oil
1 lb (½ kilo) courgettes	1 pound zucchini
1 lb (½ kilo) tomatoes, skinned and chopped	1 pound tomatoes, skinned and chopped
1 green pepper	1 green pepper
1 red pepper	1 red pepper
1 sprig fresh basil or marjoram	1 sprig fresh basil or marjoram
Sea salt	Sea salt
Freshly ground black pepper	Freshly ground black pepper

1. Cut the aubergines (eggplants) into ¼ in. (½cm) thick slices. Sprinkle with sea salt and leave for 30 minutes. (This draws out the bitterness.)
2. Meanwhile prepare the other vegetables. Finely slice the onion, crush the garlic and cut the courgettes (zucchini) into ¼ in. (½cm) thick slices, finely slice the peppers into 1 in. (2cm) long strips. Then rinse, dry and dice the aubergines (eggplants).
3. *Sauté* together in the oil the aubergines (eggplants), onions and garlic. Cook over a low heat, covered, for 10 minutes.
4. Stir in the courgettes (zucchini), tomatoes, peppers and herbs and cover. Cook for 30 minutes, stirring occasionally. Season to taste.

RICE SALAD

Serves 8 as a side dish. Supplies 2.4g protein/158 calories per portion.

Imperial (Metric)	American
½ lb (¼ kilo) long-grain brown rice	1 cupful long-grain brown rice
1 red pepper	1 red pepper
A few spring onions	A few scallions
½ cucumber	½ cucumber
4 oz (100g) button mushrooms	2 cupsful button mushrooms
2 oz (50g) sultanas	⅓ cupful golden seedless raisins

Dressing:

Imperial (Metric)	American
2 tablespoonsful olive or sunflower oil	2 tablespoonsful olive or sunflower oil
1 dessertspoonful cider or white wine vinegar	2 teaspoonsful cider or white wine vinegar
Sea salt	Sea salt
Freshly ground black pepper	Freshly ground black pepper
2 tablespoonsful chopped parsley	2 tablespoonsful chopped parsley

1. Cook the rice in boiling water until just tender. Meanwhile prepare the vegetables.
2. Finely chop the pepper, reserving a few strips for garnish. Finely chop the onions, finely dice the cucumber and slice the mushrooms.
3. Drain the rice and mix in the prepared vegetables. Stir in the sultanas.
4. In a screw-top jar, shake together the oil, vinegar and seasoning. Pour over the rice and mix in thoroughly. Sprinkle parsley over top and garnish with a few strips of red pepper.

SAVOURY RED CABBAGE

Serves 6. Supplies 2g protein/68 calories per portion.

Add vinegar and apples to preserve the colour of the cabbage — and to give a tangy flavour.

Imperial (Metric)	**American**
1 medium red cabbage	1 medium red cabbage
1 onion	1 onion
2 small cooking apples	2 small cooking apples
2 tablespoonsful red wine vinegar	2 tablespoonsful red wine vinegar
1 dessertspoonful Muscovado sugar	2 teaspoonsful Muscovado sugar
Sea salt	Sea salt
Freshly ground black pepper	Freshly ground black pepper

1. Finely shred and wash the cabbage. Finely chop the onion and peel and finely dice the apples.
2. *Sauté* the onion in the oil for 2 minutes. Stir in the apple and cabbage thoroughly.
3. Add the vinegar and an equal amount of water and the sugar. Mix in well, cover and cook for 30-40 minutes until quite tender. Season to taste.

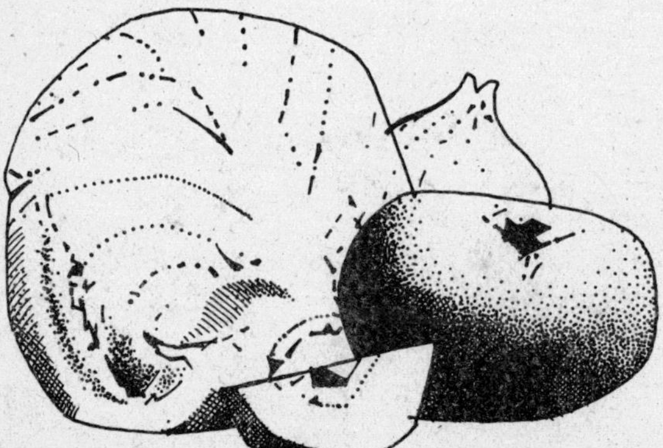

CRISPY CABBAGE SALAD

Serves 6. Supplies 2g protein/75 calories per portion.

Imperial (Metric)	American
1 small red cabbage	1 small red cabbage
1 eating apple	1 eating apple
1 large carrot	1 large carrot
1 large green pepper	1 large green pepper
4 sticks celery	4 stalks celery
4 oz (100g) button mushrooms	2 cupsful button mushrooms
2 tablespoonsful olive oil	2 tablespoonsful olive oil
Juice of half a lemon	Juice of half a lemon
Sea salt	Sea salt
Freshly ground black pepper	Freshly ground black pepper
1 tablespoonful chopped parsley	1 tablespoonful chopped parsley

1. Grate the cabbage, apple and carrot. Finely chop the pepper and celery and finely slice the mushrooms.

2. Mix together in salad bowl. Make a dressing by shaking together the oil, juice, seasoning and parsley. Pour over vegetables and toss so that all are coated.

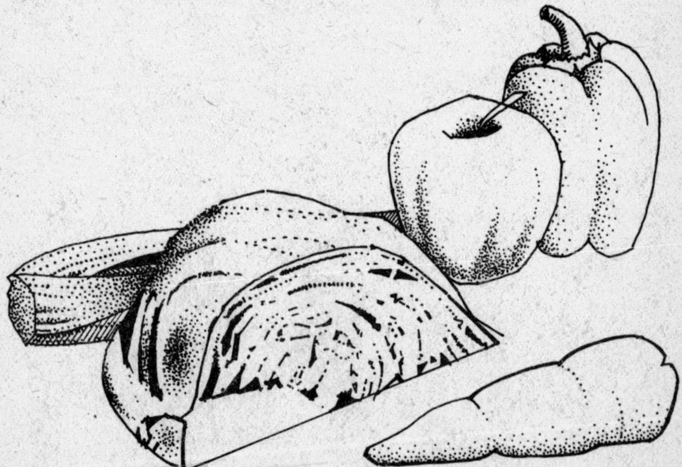

SPROUTS PURÉE

Serves 6. Supplies 3g protein/80 calories per portion.

The perfect accompaniment to Chestnut Roast (page 70).

Imperial (Metric)
1 lb (½ kilo) Brussels sprouts
2 oz (50g) butter or soft vegetable margarine
Pinch nutmeg
Freshly ground black pepper

American
1 pound Brussels sprouts
¼ cupful butter or soft vegetable margarine
Pinch nutmeg
Freshly ground black pepper

1. Prepare the sprouts and cook in a little boiling water until just tender.
2. Liquidize with a little of the cooking water, the butter and nutmeg. Beat until quite smooth and season with pepper. Use to fill centre of Chestnut Roast (page 70).

SWEDE AND CARROT PURÉE

Serves 4. Supplies 3g protein/80 calories per generous serving.

Imperial (Metric)	American
2 lb (1 kilo) swede	2 pounds rutabaga
¾ lb (350g) carrots	3 large carrots
Knob butter	Knob butter
1 tablespoonful milk	1 tablespoonful milk
Sea salt	Sea salt
Freshly ground black pepper	Freshly ground black pepper

1. Cut swede (rutabaga) into quarters. Peel and dice each quarter.
2. Scrub and slice the carrots into thin rounds. Place with the swede (rutabaga) in a large pan. Add water to come half-way up pan. Bring to the boil and then reduce heat to a steady simmer and cook for 40 minutes. The vegetables should be really soft to mash easily.
3. Drain, reserving fluid for stock. Quickly mash to a *purée* adding butter and milk. Season to taste — be liberal with the pepper. Return to pan and heat through.

TOMATO SALAD

Serves 5. Supplies 1g protein/69 calories per portion.

Imperial (Metric)	**American**
1 lb (½ kilo) tomatoes	1 pound tomatoes
1 medium onion	1 medium onion
Finely chopped fresh basil	Finely chopped fresh basil
Juice of half a lemon	Juice of half a lemon
2 tablespoonsful olive oil	2 tablespoonsful olive oil
Sea salt	Sea salt
Freshly ground black pepper	Freshly ground black pepper

1. Finely slice the tomatoes and cut the onion into fine rings.
2. Arrange together in a shallow dish. In a screw-top jar shake together the basil, lemon juice, oil and seasoning. Pour over tomatoes and onions. Chill and serve.

Note: If you cannot obtain fresh basil, parsley can be substituted.

WALDORF SALAD

Serves 6. Supplies 1.9g protein/170 calories per portion.

One of the classics of the salad table.

Imperial (Metric)
4 crisp eating apples
Juice of a lemon
1 head of celery
2 oz (50g) walnuts
2 oz (50g) raisins
4 tablespoonsful mayonnaise
Sea salt
Freshly ground black pepper

American
4 crisp eating apples
Juice of a lemon
1 head of celery
½ cupful English walnuts
⅓ cupful raisins
⅓ cupful mayonnaise
Sea salt
Freshly ground black pepper

1. Cut the cored apples into small cubes, leaving the peel on. Sprinkle with the lemon juice to prevent browning.
2. Finely chop the celery and walnuts. Mix in with the apple, add the raisins and bind together with the mayonnaise, season and chill.

WATERCRESS AND ORANGE SALAD

Serves 4. Supplies 1.5g protein/60 calories per portion.

An attractive salad which is nutritionally balanced to — the vitamin C in the orange helps the iron in the watercress to be absorbed by the body.

Imperial (Metric)	**American**
2 bunches watercress	2 bunches watercress
2 large oranges	2 large oranges
Juice of half an orange	Juice of half an orange
Pinch tarragon	Pinch tarragon
2 tablespoons olive oil	2 tablespoons olive oil

1. Wash the watercress and remove any thick stalks and yellowing leaves. Arrange on a plate.
2. Peel the oranges and cut into segments, removing the pith. Arrange on the bed of watercress.
3. Place the orange juice, tarragon and oil in a screw-top jar and shake together vigorously. Pour over the salad.

8.
SWEETS

FRESH FRUIT SALAD

Serves 4. Supplies 1g protein/150 calories per portion.

The variations are endless — choose top quality fruit and prepare as close as possible to eating to minimize loss of vitamin C from the fruits.

Imperial (Metric)	American
2 tablespoonsful clear honey	2 tablespoonsful clear honey
6 tablespoonsful warm water	½ cupful warm water
1 small bunch black grapes	1 small bunch black grapes
2 red skinned eating apples	2 red skinned eating apples
1 tablespoonful lemon juice	1 tablespoonful lemon juice
1 large orange	1 large orange
1 grapefruit	1 grapefruit
1 honeydew melon	1 honeydew melon
1 banana	1 banana

1. Dissolve the honey in the water and cool. Set aside.
2. Wash the grapes, halve and remove pips. Core and finely slice the apples. Toss in the lemon juice.
3. Peel and segment the orange and grapefruit. Cut the melon into six, then cut flesh away from peel and cut into chunks.
4. Mix all fruit together in a bowl and pour over syrup. Just before serving, finely slice the banana and add to the bowl.

DRIED FRUIT COMPOTE

Serves 4. Supplies 1.9g protein/90 calories per portion.

Imperial (Metric)

½ lb (¼ kilo) dried fruits — mix together dried apricots, figs, prunes, dried apple rings, dried peaches and pears
1 orange or lemon
Pinch nutmeg
½ teaspoonful cinnamon

American

1½ cupsful dried fruits — mix together dried apricots, figs, prunes, dried apple rings, dried peaches and pears
1 orange or lemon
Pinch nutmeg
½ teaspoonful cinnamon

1. Place dried fruit in a small saucepan, cover with cold water. Bring to the boil and then drain.
2. Cover fruit with fresh water, bring to boil, slice orange or lemon finely and add to pan with the spices. Cover and reduce heat to a steady simmer. Cook for 20 minutes. Serve warm or cold.

ROSY RED SALAD

Serves 4. Supplies just under 2g protein/85 calories per portion.

Imperial (Metric)	American
½ lb (¼ kilo) strawberries	2 cupsful strawberries
½ lb (¼ kilo) raspberries	2 cupsful raspberries
½ lb (¼ kilo) blackcurrants	2 cupsful blackcurrants
2 tablespoonsful clear, mild honey	2 tablespoonsful clear, mild honey
4 tablespoonsful water	⅓ cupful water

1. Sort and wash the fruit. Place the blackcurrants in a pan with the honey and water and simmer for a couple of minutes until just soft.

2. Remove from heat and stir in the strawberries and raspberries. Divide between four glass dishes and chill.

ALMOND PEARS

Serves 4. Supplies 4.5g protein/176 calories per portion.

Fairly high in protein because of the almond filling. Eat these after a grain or pulse based dish to balance the protein.

Imperial (Metric)
4 oz (100g) ground almonds
Grated rind and juice of a lemon
Grated rind and juice of an orange
Pinch cinnamon
4 Comice pears

American
1 cupful ground almonds
Grated rind and juice of a lemon
Grated rind and juice of an orange
Pinch cinnamon
4 Comice pears

1. Mix together the almonds, rind and juice of the lemon, the orange rind and the cinnamon.

2. Carefully peel and core the pears. Stuff the centres with the almond mixture and pour over orange juice making sure it coats all the fruit. Cover and bake at 350°F/180°C (Gas Mark 4) for 20 minutes.

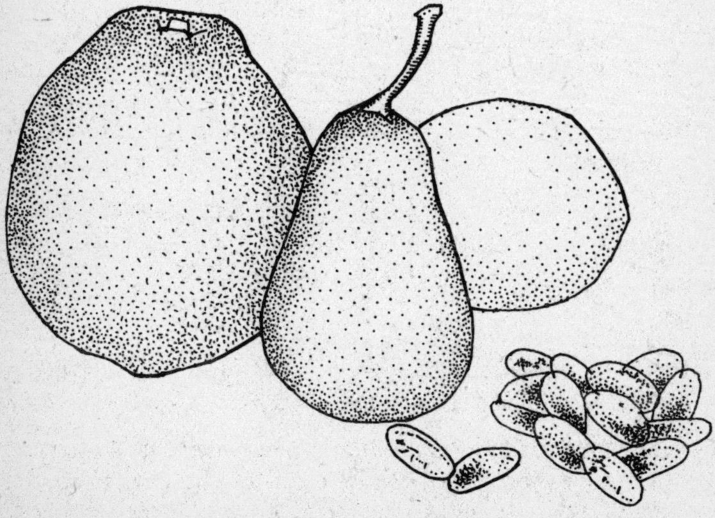

LATTICED PEAR SLICE

Serves 4. Supplies 5.7g protein/240 calories.

A naturally sweet and attractive dessert — serve after a pulse or a nut based main course to make the most of the protein in the pastry.

Pastry:

Imperial (Metric)	**American**
2 oz (50g) soft vegetable margarine	4 tablespoonsful soft vegetable margarine
4 oz (100g) wholemeal flour	1 cupful wholewheat flour
1 oz (25g) light Muscovado sugar	2 tablespoonsful light Muscovado sugar
¼ teaspoonful cinnamon	¼ teaspoonful cinnamon
Grated rind of a lemon	Grated rind of a lemon
Cold water to mix	Cold water to mix

Filling:

Imperial (Metric)	**American**
4 firm pears	4 firm pears
1 oz (25g) sultanas	¼ cupful golden seedless raisins
1 tablespoonful lemon juice	1 tablespoonful lemon juice

1. Rub margarine into flour until mixture resembles fine breadcrumbs.
2. Stir in the sugar, cinnamon and lemon rind. Add just enough water to bind to a soft dough.
3. Roll out and line a 7 in. (18cm) flan dish, reserving a few strips of pastry for decoration.
4. Peel and roughly chop the pears, mix with the sultanas and lemon juice and arrange evenly in flan case.
5. Roll out pastry trimmings and cut into several fine strips. Arrange in a lattice on top of the pears. Brush with a little milk and bake at 400°F/200°C (Gas Mark 6) for 35 minutes. Serve hot or cold.

PEAR AND ORANGE CRUNCH

Serves 5. Supplies 3g protein/300 calories per portion.

Imperial (Metric)
2 oz (50g) soft vegetable margarine
2 oz (50g) wholemeal flour
2 oz (50g) rolled oats
2 oz (50g) dessicated coconut
1 oz (25g) raw cane Demerara sugar
Rind and juice of an orange
4 firm pears
3 oz (75g) sultanas

American
¼ cupful soft vegetable margarine
½ cupful wholewheat flour
½ cupful rolled oats
⅔ cupful dessicated coconut
2 tablespoonsful raw cane Demerara sugar
Rind and juice of an orange
4 firm pears
½ cupful golden seedless raisins

1. Rub fat into flour and oats. Stir in the coconut and sugar and the orange rind.
2. Peel and roughly chop the pears. Mix with the sultanas (golden seedless raisins) and orange juice and place in base of an ovenproof dish.
3. Cover with crumble mixture and bake at 400°F/200°C (Gas Mark 6) for 30 minutes, until fruit is soft and topping golden brown.

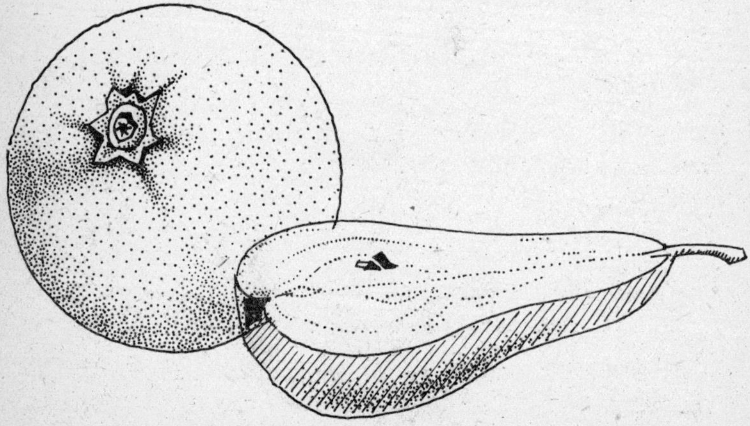

APPLE CRUMBLE

Serves 4. Supplies 4g protein/260 calories per portion.

Substituting seeds and nuts for some flour gives a protein-balanced topping which is also less sweet than normal. Substitute plums, rhubarb or blackberries as liked.

Imperial (Metric)	American
2 oz (50g) soft vegetable margarine	¼ cupful soft vegetable margarine
2 oz (50g) wholemeal flour	½ cupful wholewheat flour
2 oz (50g) rolled oats	½ cupful rolled oats
1 tablespoonful sunflower seeds	1 tablespoonful sunflower seeds
1 tablespoonful finely chopped almonds	1 tablespoonful finely chopped almonds
1 oz (25g) Demerara sugar	2 tablespoonsful Demerara sugar
1½ lb (¾ kilo) cooking apples	1½ pounds cooking apples
1 tablespoonful clear honey	1 tablespoonful clear honey

1. Rub margarine into flour and oats. Stir in the seeds, nuts and sugar.
2. Peel and finely slice the apples. Place in an ovenproof dish and dribble honey over. Add a tablespoonful of water.
3. Cover with crumble topping and bake at 400°F/200°C (Gas Mark 6) for 25 minutes until fruit is soft and topping golden.

BAKED APPLES

Serves 4. Supplies just under 1g protein/170 calories each.

Choose dried fruit to stuff the centres of apples for a low-protein sweet.

Imperial (Metric)	**American**
4 even-sized cooking apples	4 even-sized cooking apples
4 oz (100g) mixed dried fruit	⅔ cupful mixed dried fruit
2 tablespoonsful clear honey	2 tablespoonsful clear honey

1. Core the apples and slit skins in a ring half-way down the apple.
2. Place apples in shallow ovenproof dish with few tablespoons water in base.
3. Stuff the centres with the dried fruit. Dribble honey over top of the stuffed centre.
4. Bake in pre-heated oven 400°F/200°C (Gas Mark 6) for around 35-40 minutes until apples are just soft.

Variation: As a change from the honey and fruit filling, stuff each apple with 1½ tablespoonsful mincemeat. The protein and calorie count remains the same.

FRUIT CHARLOTTE

Serves 4. Supplies 2.5g protein/260 calories per portion.

Imperial (Metric)	American
1½ lb (675g) cooking apples	4 cooking apples
4 oz (100g) wholemeal breadcrumbs	2 cupsful wholewheat breadcrumbs
2 oz (50g) butter or soft vegetable margarine	¼ cupful butter or soft vegetable margarine
2 oz (50g) raw cane Demerara sugar	⅓ cupful raw cane Demerara sugar
Pinch cinnamon	Pinch cinnamon

1. Peel, core and slice apples and cook with a tablespoonful water over a very low heat until quite soft and pulpy. Beat to a smooth *purée* and cool. Sweeten if necessary.
2. Place breadcrumbs and butter in saucepan and cook gently until breadcrumbs turn a crispy golden brown, stirring continually to prevent burning. Stir in the sugar and cinnamon.
3. Divide apple *purée* between four sundae glasses and smooth over. Top with the breadcrumb mixture and chill.

Note: Any cooked and cooled fruit of your choice may be substituted for the apples.

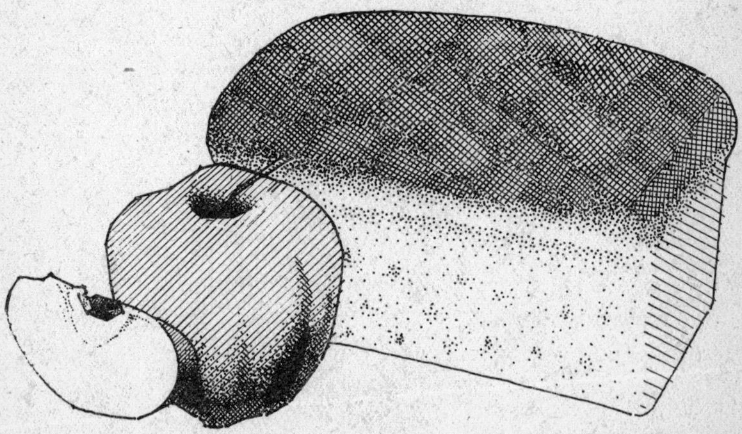

GRAPEFRUIT AND MELON REFRESHER

Serves 3. Supplies 1.7g protein/46 calories per portion.

Imperial (Metric)	American
1 ripe melon (honeydew or ogen)	1 ripe melon (honeydew or ogen)
1 large grapefruit	1 large grapefruit
Juice of 1 lime	Juice of 1 lime

1. Halve the melon and remove the seeds. Cut the flesh into cubes.
2. Peel the grapefruit and cut into segments. Mix with the melon and add the lime juice. Leave to chill for at least 30 minutes before serving in glass dishes.

Note: While grapefruit and melon are popular 'starters', this also makes a delicious dessert.

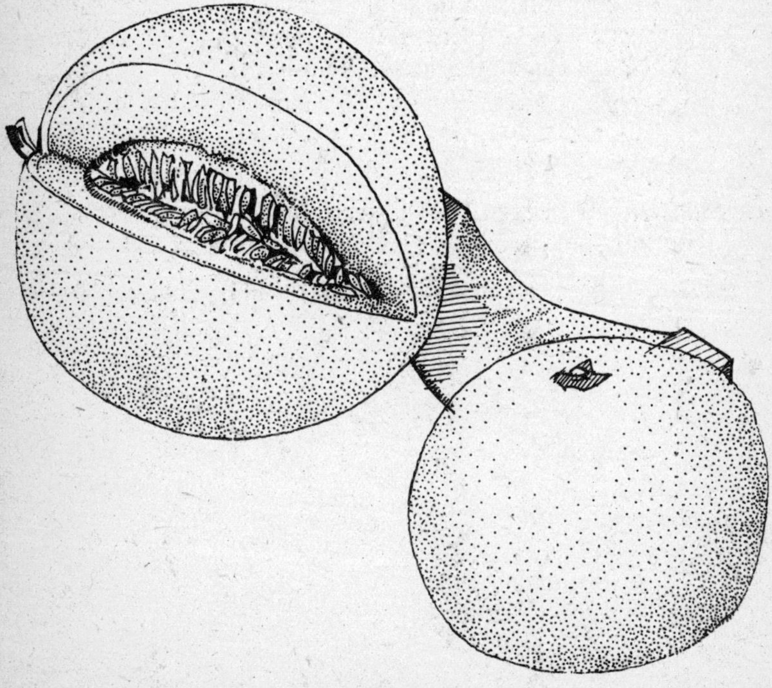

APRICOT FOOL

Serves 4. Supplies 5.4g protein/135 calories per portion.

To keep the protein content of this dessert down gelatine is omitted and just one egg white is used. The result is a thick tangy *purée*. Dried apricots are a very good source of minerals.

Imperial (Metric)	**American**
4 oz (100g) dried apricots, soaked overnight	1½ cupsful dried apricots, soaked overnight
Grated rind and juice of a lemon	Grated rind and juice of a lemon
1 tablespoonsful clear honey	1 tablespoonsful clear honey
¼ pint (150ml) natural yogurt	⅔ cupful natural yogurt
1 egg white	1 egg white

1. Strain the apricots and make up their soaking water to ½ pint (300ml)/1⅓ cupsful. Place the fruit, water, lemon juice and rind in a pan and cook for 20 minutes until soft.
2. Liquidize and cool.
3. Add honey and yogurt to *purée*, blending in well.
4. Stiffly whisk the egg white and gently fold into the apricot *purée*. Pour into four individual glasses or a large bowl and chill.

Variation: Prunes, or a fresh fruit *purée*, could be used in place of the apricots.

INDEX